# ROOTED IN LOVE

The **Rt Revd and Rt Hon. Dame Sarah Mullally DBE** is Bishop of London. Before her ordination, she was Chief Nursing Officer in the Department of Health. She was made Dame Commander of the British Empire in 2005 for her contribution to nursing and midwifery. Her previous books include *A Good Advent* (SPCK, 2018).

# ROOTED IN LOVE

Lent reflections on life in Christ

Edited and introduced by
Sarah Mullally

First published in Great Britain in 2020

Society for Promoting Christian Knowledge
36 Causton Street
London SW1P 4ST
www.spck.org.uk

*British Library Cataloguing-in-Publication Data*
A catalogue record for this book is available from the British Library

ISBN 978–0–281–08488–3
eBook ISBN 978–0–281–08487–6

Typeset by Manila Typesetting Company
First printed in Great Britain by Jellyfish Print Solutions
Subsequently digitally printed in Great Britain

eBook by Manila Typesetting Company

Produced on paper from sustainable forests

# Contents

# Contents

## Part 4
## BECOMING MORE CHRIST-LIKE

# Contents

## Part 5
## LIVING A CHRIST-CENTRED LIFE

# Acknowledgements

I am grateful for the bishops who serve the London diocese (sometimes referred to as the London College of Bishops), who have together written these reflections.

**The Rt Revd Jonathan Baker** is Bishop of Fulham, providing alternative episcopal oversight in Greater London. His wealth of experience includes having previously served as Bishop of Ebbsfleet.

**The Rt Revd Pete Broadbent** has been Bishop of Willesden since 2001, having previously served as Archdeacon of Northolt and Vicar of Trinity St Michael, Harrow.

**The Rt Revd Dr Joanne Grenfell**, Bishop of Stepney, is our lead bishop for social responsibility and was previously Archdeacon in the Diocese of Portsmouth.

**The Rt Revd Dr Ric Thorpe**, Bishop of Islington, is free from territorial responsibilities so that he can support London's church growth strategy. Before this he served as Rector of St Paul's Shadwell.

**The Rt Revd Dr Graham Tomlin**, Bishop of Kensington, joined from St Mellitus College, where he was Dean for eight years and continues to serve as President.

**The Rt Revd Rob Wickham**, Bishop of Edmonton, was previously Rector of St John at Hackney and Area Dean of Hackney.

## Acknowledgements

As a team they bring a huge range of gifts with which to serve our city, and I hugely value their partnership in the gospel.

The Rt Revd and Rt Hon. Dame Sarah Mullally DBE

# Introduction

> I pray that, according to the riches of his glory, he may grant that you may be strengthened in your inner being with power through his Spirit, and that Christ may dwell in your hearts through faith, as you are being rooted and grounded in love. I pray that you may have the power to comprehend, with all the saints, what is the breadth and length and height and depth, and to know the love of Christ that surpasses knowledge, so that you may be filled with all the fullness of God.
> (Eph. 3.16–17)

It is when life is most strained that the strength of our faith shines through. We are still emerging from a time of great strain and trauma in the wake of the coronavirus pandemic. Our isolation was more prolonged than many had ever experienced, and the challenges to our way of life more profound than we could have imagined. The enforced physical distancing from others and the pressure that this created on life at work and at home has been immense. The full economic impact of all this on individuals and on the economy is still emerging.

In the midst of the fallout, Christians are called to continue living together in the hope of the gospel. We seek to serve those in our communities with practical care, wise words and loving dispositions. There have been many opportunities for Christians to bless their communities in recent months, but the demands of the season ahead are considerable too.

To take one example, the economic consequences of COVID-19 are likely to have the greatest impact on those who were already on the margins. In the light of this the Archbishop of Canterbury said last Easter that we have a choice as a nation, as a society and as a world: 'Do we take hold of our destiny and make sure that these differences are mitigated, abolished where possible, or do we just let things happen, do we let the market rule? In which case, there will be enormous suffering.'[1]

This is just one challenge of many. And such challenges raise the question 'How do we keep going?' More than that, how do we do more than simply cling on to our faith but grow in it? In this context, the letter to the Ephesians is an incredibly rich resource for us. It maps out a path that helps us to walk into the unknown with confidence.

The English poet Samuel Taylor Coleridge said that the letter to the Ephesians is 'the divinest composition of man'.[2] It soars up to mountain peaks of spiritual truth and takes time to look over them with awe and wonder. In this letter the apostle Paul delights in the blessings of the gospel, before outlining its demands on us as a community. Our focus is on how he links the two together, how he points us to the fuel we need for the journey. We are as much in need of this insight today as Paul's original hearers were.

The blessings of the first half of the book are rich and wonderful. In it Paul tells us that in Christ we are chosen by the Father (1.4–6), redeemed by the Son (1.7–12) and sealed by the Spirit (1.13–14) for an unshakeable eternal inheritance, all for his praise and glory (1.6, 12, 14). We reach the kind of theological equivalent of scaling Mount Everest. If the way in which God has designed the natural world is awe-inspiring, how much more his grand design of the story of salvation.

## Coping with chaos

If the blessings of the gospel were extensive, so were its demands. From chapter 4 onwards Paul addresses lies, anger, gossip, inability to forgive, sexual immorality, marriage, family strife, unfair working practices and spiritual attack, all of which threaten to tear apart the life of the church and shroud the community in division and slander.

Just as in our present time, living out the gospel in a fractured world was hugely challenging. The Ephesian Christians needed energizing encouragement in their hearts that would enable them to persevere. We need the same in our time. Paul's argument is that this is available in the supernatural knowledge of God's love for us in Christ.

The word 'love' is used so commonly in everyday speech that the profound mysteries to which the love of Christ refers can easily be eclipsed. To love a chocolate bar, a novel or Jesus Christ may all trip off the tongue in the same conversation, but some uses of the word refer more to a temporary whim, while others tend towards a more permanent affection and commitment.

As reflecting a terminological instability, what we call love for other people can also veer towards being more fickle than firm. The *Love Island* television series was a case in point. The dating reality show, cancelled because of the COVID-19 pandemic, saw contestants living in isolation together in a villa in Mallorca under constant video surveillance. Footage of how they dealt with regularly being forced to 're-couple' proved an unexpected hit. In one series, a contestant on the show, keen to demonstrate his willingness to swap partners said, 'We're on Love Island, not . . . Loyalty Island.'[3] For him, love was as changeable as the wind, based mainly on what he perceived he could get out of a relationship.

The love of Christ, however, points us to something deeper. In God we see a love based on the glory of giving rather than on what we can get. In fact, in Christ we see God giving his best to those who deserved it the least. The rebellious are shown the riches of mercy. Objects of wrath are raised up to the heavenly realms. The spiritually dead are made alive (Eph. 2.2–6). And all this is achieved through an act of incomparable humility: Christ left his home of heavenly adoration to face earthly hostility, and his sacrifice on the cross secured our salvation.

In an interview a few years ago, the novelist Rose Tremain spoke movingly about the absence of love that she had felt growing up. Her father had walked out on the family, and she and her sister were packed off to boarding school. As she became an adult, she tried to reach out to her father, who had broken off all contact, to no avail. The rejection was so extreme that, even when she sent him books that she had written, he would return them unread.

The only person that she could rely on for affection was her nanny. She said, 'In some miraculous way, maybe because I was shown love by Nan, I was all right. I had a template for how one might love.'[4]

It is such a 'template of love' that Paul wants to place in the hearts of the Ephesian believers. The difference is that this template is one that is richer than even our closest companions on earth can muster. When Rose was sent away, even the love of her nanny was stolen. The love that Paul points us to is a permanent, passionate love – love even for the unlovely. This in turn unlocks in us a passionate love for him and for others.

## Strengthened in your inner being

Paul knows that it is critical for this church to be strengthened in a knowledge of this incredible love. So, quite unusually in the Jewish tradition, he gets down on his knees to pray. He cannot make it any clearer that what he is about to say is of the highest importance and beyond our natural ability to obtain. It can be summarized like this: the supernatural work of God that made the Ephesians *spiritually* one family is the only thing that can enable them to act *practically* like a family.

They need the help of the Holy Spirit (v. 16), so that Christ becomes for them more than an intellectual curiosity, on the one hand, or a formal pastime, on the other. Instead he must have access to the very control centre of their being, their hearts (v. 17). It is when their whole being is 'rooted' like a tree in him and the foundation of their hearts is 'established' in the love of God in Christ (Eph. 2.4), that they will be able to grow into the maturity that will enable them to persevere despite the trials they face.

One reason why this is so important is that life has a habit of exposing us to challenges that cast a shadow over any superficial understanding of the love of God in Christ. We find ourselves asking the questions that run through the Psalms in times of trouble: How long? Why? Where are you? It is only this deep, rich experience of what God's love is really like that will enable us to continue to hope in God – to not let the shadows of our trials distract us from the brilliance of the Son of God.

It is knowing Christ, to quote Augustine, as the 'true happiness of life' that will sustain us.[5] It is yearning for the one in whose presence there is only joy and at whose right hand are eternal pleasures (Ps. 16.11) that will spur us on. It is trusting Christ as the one who endured suffering so that he might shower blessing on those who trust him that will help us to persevere.[6] It is a knowledge so rich and deep that there are always more depths to explore. As one of the old Sankey hymns encourages us:

It passeth knowledge, that dear love of thine,
My Saviour, Jesus; yet this soul of mine
Would of thy love in all its breadth and length,
Its height and depth, its everlasting strength,
    Know more and more.

## Growing in community

Having already made it clear that this is in the realm of a divine gift, Paul also emphasizes that we need other Christians too – we are engaged in an endeavour with all the saints (v. 18).

This severely challenges our individualistic culture and often individualistic faith. There are times when the injunctions to follow our heart and to find ourselves push us out of our comfort zones to attempt more for God. Yet it is hard to carry each other's burdens (Gal. 6.2), to pray for one another (James 5.16), to encourage one another (1 Thess. 1.18) or to forgive one another (Col. 3.13) if our faith is expressed alone or only occasionally with others whom we barely know. As John the Baptist discovered when he was imprisoned, isolation can make us question even our strongest convictions (Luke 7.19–23). Our growth with Christ requires others. The implication of Ephesians 3.18 is that to try to grow our relationship with him without involving others will leave us lacking in power and maturity. God encourages us to harness the wisdom that only fellow brothers and sisters in Christ can bring us.

This is the task in which we dare to engage in this book. We long for God to do more than simply increase our knowledge, for him to inflame our hearts as we reflect together on what it means to be the Church in a new season.

The book is arranged to point us first to the Christ we serve (Part 1), then to our calling and baptism into the body of Christ (Parts 2 and 3) and finally to the how and the what of growing more like Christ (Parts 4 and 5). For this reason, the devotions are designed to be read sequentially over the forty days of the Lent period. To honour the encouragement of Paul to seek power 'together with all the saints', we encourage you to gather with others or to share your thoughts with friends. We are confident, however, that each devotion stands alone as a source of encouragement, prayer and biblical wisdom, however you choose to use it.

The road ahead for all of us may be unknown, but God has made it abundantly clear that we need to persevere. May he bless you richly as you seek and savour the love of his Son in the Scriptures.

## Notes

1 Ed Thornton, 'We have given guidance, not instruction, says Welby on *Andrew Marr Show*', *Church Times*, 15 April 2020, <www.churchtimes.co.uk/articles/2020/17-april/news/uk/we-have-given-guidance-not-instruction-says-welby-on-andrew-marr-show>.

2 Quoted by Peter T. O'Brien, *The Letter to the Ephesians* (Grand Rapids, MI: Eerdmans, 1999), p. 1.

3 'We're all hopelessly addicted – so can some of Britain's top academics explain Love Island's gruesome fascination?', *Daily Mail*, 8 June 2018, <https://www.dailymail.co.uk/femail/article-5822853/Britains-academics-explain-Love-Islands-gruesome-fascination.html>.

4 Rachel Sylvester and Alice Thomson, 'Rose Tremain interview: "Everyone is rushing to their own identity corner. It divides society"', *The Times*, 6 October 2018, <https://www.thetimes.co.uk/article/rose-tremain-interview-everyone-is-rushing-to-their-own-identity-corner-it-divides-society-djcj8kxrk>.

5 Augustine, *On Christian Doctrine*, ch. 29.

6 Augustine, *City of God*, bk 22, ch. 24.

7 <www.hymnal.net/en/hymn/h/154>.

Part I

# THE CHRIST WE SERVE

# 1

# The Word made flesh

In the beginning was the Word, and the Word was with God, and the Word was God. He was in the beginning with God. All things came into being through him, and without him not one thing came into being. What has come into being in him was life, and the life was the light of all people. The light shines in the darkness, and the darkness did not overcome it.

There was a man sent from God, whose name was John. He came as a witness to testify to the light, so that all might believe through him. He himself was not the light, but he came to testify to the light. The true light, which enlightens everyone, was coming into the world.

He was in the world, and the world came into being through him; yet the world did not know him. He came to what was his own, and his own people did not accept him. But to all who received him, who believed in his name, he gave power to become children of God, who were born, not of blood or of the will of the flesh or of the will of man, but of God.

And the Word became flesh and lived among us, and we have seen his glory, the glory as of a father's only son, full of grace and truth. (John testified to him and cried out, 'This was he of whom I said, "He who comes

after me ranks ahead of me because he was before me."') From his fullness we have all received, grace upon grace. The law indeed was given through Moses; grace and truth came through Jesus Christ. No one has ever seen God. It is God the only Son, who is close to the Father's heart, who has made him known.
(John 1.1–18)

This life holds many mysteries, many unanswered questions. We look into a dark night sky and marvel at our smallness in a vast universe; we cry agonizing tears when we lose friends and family, or when a relationship fails; we wonder about the meaning of life, or freedom, or suffering. At the heart of this famous text, read every Christmas in churches across the world, is the idea that the answer to the deepest mysteries of our lives, even the entire cosmos, is found not in a philosophical idea or a scientific discovery, but in a person. Within just a few decades of Jesus' life, when there were still people around who had known him in the flesh, we find this remarkable claim. Jesus, the controversial rabbi from Nazareth in Galilee, who had a brief public career and was quickly silenced by the Roman authorities in Jerusalem, is in fact the unveiling of the mystery at the heart of the universe. He was 'in the beginning with God' – there at the very start, even before the Big Bang. 'All things came into being through him' – the whole of creation, in its original unfallen state, somehow carries the stamp of his nature and character. 'In him was life, and the life was the light of all people' – the very life that breathes through all of us, the light that fills each day, reflected to us from the sun, all comes originally from the Father, refracted through him. 'No one has ever seen God', we are reminded, but 'the only Son, who is close to the Father's heart, who has made him known'.

In the time when John's Gospel was written, Stoic philosophers among others often wrote of the *Logos*, or the 'Word'. It was thought to be a kind of divine wisdom or logic that permeated the whole of creation and that all philosophers were seeking after. The fourth Gospel makes the bold claim that this wisdom, for which all the world's philosophers were searching, the secret mystery at the heart of the universe – is revealed to us in Jesus Christ, the 'Word made flesh'. As St Paul put it later, writing to the Christians in Colossae, Jesus is the one 'in whom are hidden all the treasures of wisdom and knowledge' (Col. 2.3).

Yet this is a strange revelation, one that doesn't immediately give us neat answers. Jesus may have been the 'Word . . . made flesh' (KJV), but that very human flesh hid the presence of the Word, and so many missed it: 'He came to what was his own, and his own people did not accept him.' The God who remains veiled from us is revealed in and through the ordinary human flesh of Jesus of Nazareth. We don't always find the immediate answers to our questions, but we are assured that those answers are hidden in Christ for those who follow him. We are told that 'all who received him, who believed in his name, he gave power to become children of God'; in other words, we are promised that if we seek every day to walk trustfully in his steps, staying close to him, following his way, we will find what we are looking for. We may not know what the future holds, but we know who holds it in his hands, and those are hands we can trust.

## Action

As we proceed through this book, starting with these reflections on the Christ we serve, this text reminds us to look around us each day for signs of his presence in the compassion of strangers, in the sacrifices made by others, in the pages of Scripture and in bread and wine. It also tells us to bring our questions, our wonderings and our fears to Jesus, in whom are found all the treasures of wisdom and knowledge.

## Prayer

God our Father, we thank you that you have revealed yourself and your love for us in your Son Jesus Christ. Even though we struggle with many questions and hidden mysteries, we trust you that in Christ are hidden all the treasures of wisdom and knowledge. Help us to trust him, to turn to him with all our questions and to seek to learn his way, that we may grow in wisdom and maturity day by day. Amen.

# 2

# If you are the Son of God

Jesus, full of the Holy Spirit, returned from the Jordan and was led by the Spirit in the wilderness, where for forty days he was tempted by the devil. He ate nothing at all during those days, and when they were over, he was famished. The devil said to him, 'If you are the Son of God, command this stone to become a loaf of bread.' Jesus answered him, 'It is written, "One does not live by bread alone."'

Then the devil led him up and showed him in an instant all the kingdoms of the world. And the devil said to him, 'To you I will give their glory and all this authority; for it has been given over to me, and I give it to anyone I please. If you, then, will worship me, it will all be yours.' Jesus answered him, 'It is written,

"Worship the Lord your God,

and serve only him."'

Then the devil took him to Jerusalem, and placed him on the pinnacle of the temple, saying to him, 'If you are the Son of God, throw yourself down from here, for it is written,

"He will command his angels concerning you,

to protect you",

and

"On their hands they will bear you up,
   so that you will not dash your foot against a stone".'
Jesus answered him, 'It is said, "Do not put the Lord your
God to the test."' When the devil had finished every
test, he departed from him until an opportune time.
(Luke 4.1–13)

If I wanted to survey all the kingdoms of Stepney Area,
where I live and work, there are three towers that I could be
led up. From the vertiginous heights of One Canada Square,
often known as the Canary Wharf Tower, I would see across
the East End and beyond. There's no public viewing tower,
so I would need to beg a favour from one of the global com-
panies that occupy the upper floors. With banking, business
and insurance interests looking over my shoulder, I could
survey the magnificent vista and feel that I have oversight of
the many smaller means of production, exchange, commu-
nication and service which keep London – and the world –
running. Perhaps I would pray for them all while I was up
there. That's what bishops are meant to do, isn't it?

If I wanted the perspective of religion alongside that of
finance, I might be led to the tower of St Dunstan's, Stepney, mother church of the East End, which has witnessed
to faith in Jesus Christ since before the current building's
tenth-century foundations. The Church of England can
feel as if it struggles for relevance in secular, multicultural
Britain, and my corner of the East End, Stepney, has been
and is a home for people of all faiths, especially displaced,
transient communities from Christianity, Judaism and
Islam. With so little agreement about values and traditions,

all voices of faith can find it hard to be heard above the clamour of fragmented postmodern views. Standing at the top of St Dunstan's tower, which is twice the size of the local mosque's minaret, with my feet firmly planted in the footsteps of previous bishops of Stepney, surely here I would feel confident in what my faith can offer to the capital and the world beyond.

Or I could be taken to the helicopter pad hanging out over Whitechapel Road on the giant blue Lego blocks of the Royal London Hospital. I'd rather go as a spectator than be rushed there by helicopter, but if I were in the unfortunate position of being an emergency patient, I'd be glad to arrive at this pinnacle of modern trauma medicine – I'd be in the best hands, wouldn't I?

Faced by the devil and led up to his own high place, Jesus refuses to find his sustenance in bread made from stones. He rejects the glory and authority that are promised him if he were to accept the world's adulation and worship anything other than the true God. He resists demonstrating his invincibility by throwing himself from the devil's high place. The Son of God is no Superman.

Money. Religion. Health. Idolatry comes in different forms. Jesus resists them all, choosing instead to point only towards the authority of the heavenly Father, with whom he is one. In our own forty days of Lenten wilderness, we examine the ways in which we are tempted to worship money, to find false gods and to seek immortality.

Jesus asks us to turn with him away from the tempting heights of worldly gain and to worship and serve only the one true God.

## Action

Search the internet for vistas of a landmark tower. Use satellite and aerial imagery to explore different views and angles. Or, if you are able and live in a suitable area, walk to the highest point in your neighbourhood. Explore the feelings that you have there. Who holds power? What is being valued in each view? How is God speaking to you about what you value and what you perhaps idolize? Ask God what you need to gain and to give up so that you can worship the one true God.

## Prayer

Lord, when I am tempted
to worship worldly power,
to idolize my own ministry
and to believe that I am invincible,
take away my fear of insignificance,
of irrelevance,
and of death.
Bring me not to mountain tops
but to the foot of the cross;
that there I may see in Christ's suffering
the breadth and length and height and depth
of your abundant love.
Amen.

# 3

# Who is this Jesus?

On that day, when evening had come, he said to them, 'Let us go across to the other side.' And leaving the crowd behind, they took him with them in the boat, just as he was. Other boats were with him. A great windstorm arose, and the waves beat into the boat, so that the boat was already being swamped. But he was in the stern, asleep on the cushion; and they woke him up and said to him, 'Teacher, do you not care that we are perishing?' He woke up and rebuked the wind, and said to the sea, 'Peace! Be still!' Then the wind ceased, and there was a dead calm. He said to them, 'Why are you afraid? Have you still no faith?' And they were filled with great awe and said to one another, 'Who then is this, that even the wind and the sea obey him?' (Mark 4.35–41)

In the Hebrew Scriptures, it is God alone who has the power to subdue the stormy seas. In creation, God sets limits around the waters, bringing order out of chaos. God tells Job that it is He 'who shut in the sea with doors when it burst out from the womb' (Job 38.8). The psalmist praises the God of salvation, 'silence the roaring of the seas, the roaring of their waves', and 'he made the storm be still, and the waves of the sea were hushed' (Pss 65.7; 107.29). But, despite God's mastery over wind and storm, the sea remains, for many of the biblical writers, a place of threat and danger. Leviathan dwells there. Describing his vision of heaven, of the new Jerusalem, St John the Divine says that 'the sea was no more' (Rev. 21.1).

In the opening chapters of St Mark's Gospel, the sea – the Sea of Galilee – has already been a place of encounter with Jesus, of his call and of the beginning of a new life. It is by the sea that Jesus calls, first, Simon and Andrew and then James and John. It is by the sea that a crowd presses on Jesus, almost crushing him. He heals many and the unclean spirits fall down before him and cries out, 'You are the Son of God!' (Mark 3.11). They are the first to recognize him as such and to accord him this title, which points to his divinity. Now, in Mark chapter 4, it is Jesus who does what God alone can do. He calms the wind and the waves, and causes the storm to cease. He rebukes the wind just as he had rebuked the unclean spirit in chapter 1 (St Mark uses exactly the same word). Then, those who saw the spirit cast out were amazed, and asked themselves, 'What is this? A new teaching – with authority! He commands even the unclean spirits, and they obey him' (Mark 1.27). Now the disciples are filled with awe, and they ask, 'Who then is this, that even the wind and the sea obey him?' (Mark 4.41). We can see (even if the disciples cannot) where St Mark is leading us. Every word, every deed in these early chapters help the readers of his Gospel to understand that in Jesus nothing less than the presence and power of God is at work.

Jesus contrasts the faith that the disciples should have (but that they lack) with the fear that they all too clearly demonstrate. Faith and fear form a pair of opposites throughout St Mark's Gospel. In chapter 6, the disciples are again in a boat at sea, this time struggling against a headwind: Jesus appears to them, walking on the water, and says, 'do not be afraid' (v. 50). The Gospel ends – famously, in its most reliable ending at least – with women at the tomb who, rather than having faith that Jesus has risen, flee from the tomb and say nothing to anyone 'for they were afraid' (Mark 16.8).

To read St Mark's Gospel, then, is to accept the evangelist's invitation to be a disciple of the Lord who has faith, not fear: faith in Jesus who stills the storm, faith in Jesus who is so filled with the fullness of the divine power and authority that we know him to be nothing less than God; faith in Jesus who is truly risen and goes before us into Galilee, that is, into the world of our own storm-filled lives and experience, where Jesus alone can bring peace and banish fear.

St Augustine, reflecting on this passage, suggests that the episode at sea signifies the drama of the Christian life. All of us who are God's children embark with Christ on a life that is full of dangerous storms. So it is that we must learn to trust Christ daily, who alone can bring us home into safe harbour.

## Action

What are you afraid of? Where do you need Jesus to still the storm and speak a word of peace today?

## Prayer

Part of a prayer of St Jane de Chantal (1572–1641) entitled simply 'Christ':

Be within me every part – in my mind, my voice, my heart – In my mouth, on my lips, even in my fingertips. Christ be in my eyes and ears – to bless my joys, to calm my fears. Amen.

# 4

# Who do you say I am?

Jesus went on with his disciples to the villages of Caesarea Philippi; and on the way he asked his disciples, 'Who do people say that I am?' And they answered him, 'John the Baptist; and others, Elijah; and still others, one of the prophets.' He asked them, 'But who do you say that I am?' Peter answered him, 'You are the Messiah.' And he sternly ordered them not to tell anyone about him. (Mark 8.27–30)

The most important question we could ever ask is 'Who is Jesus?' Why? Because it affects our ultimate destiny and that is as important as life itself. If Jesus is who he claimed to be, then the sooner we come to terms with that the better. And if he *is* the Messiah, then that truth changes everything in terms of how we live our lives now.

Jesus asks the disciples, 'Who do people say that I am?' The disciples respond with a variety of common answers of the time. There were and there are still so many different opinions about who Jesus is.

- Most are based on a lack of knowledge – there's plenty of evidence in Scripture of who Jesus is, but many people can't be bothered to find out or they fear the consequences of finding out and so they don't start.

- Some opinions are based on what people have been told by others – such as the views of other faiths such as Islam or Judaism, or a perspective that has been handed down within a family.
- Some opinions are based on real enquiry but an enquiry rooted itself in preconceived notions.

But Jesus always makes it personal. He asks them, 'But what about you? Who do you say that I am?' He digs past the layers of excuses, ignorance or untruths and lays bare our hearts. Deep down, then, who is Jesus?

I'll never forget being confronted with that question when I was nineteen. I was invited to St John's Harborne church in Birmingham. Nick Cuthbert was preaching. I can't remember Nick's talk (sorry, Nick!), but I do remember experiencing Jesus in my mind's eye. I saw Jesus covered in things with which I'd wrapped him up in my mind – explaining away the miracles, bringing my own moral perspective to living life – but I felt him saying, 'It's not about that stuff – it's about me!' And he came towards me and embraced me, and I experienced his deep and profound love for me. That's how discovering Jesus started for me.

To Jesus' question, Peter declares, 'You are the Messiah.' In Matthew's account he goes on to say, 'the son of the living God' (Matt. 16.15). Wow! Peter realizes something profound – you are more than human, you are the one sent from above, you are not just an angel but of a God himself! And you are *the* Son, not just *a* son.

The magnitude of this realization is enormous. For Jesus, it marks a shift. He tells them not to tell anyone yet, but from this moment he begins to talk about his own destiny on the cross and his resurrection, and about following him no matter what the cost. And it changes everything for Peter too – it's literally an OMG moment – a revelation of who Jesus really is.

And it changes everything for us too. If he is the Christ, it means that we must not reject him but follow him. If he is the Son of God, then we must bow down in our hearts and worship him, putting aside a distorted image of Jesus in favour of who he really is – the one in whom we are called to put our trust. The one whom God has chosen. The one who invites us to follow him.

## Action

Mark invites us to ask the same question about Jesus. And the answer will change us for ever too.

1 Ask yourself this question afresh: who is Jesus? What does he mean for you?
2 How does acknowledging his identity affect your life? Are you living in the light of its truth? How can you follow him more? What idols do you need to put aside?
3 Who might you put this question to? 'Who is Jesus?' may be the most important question you could ask them.

## Prayer

Lord Jesus, thank you that you are the Christ, the chosen one of God, who loved me and gave himself for me. May the truth of who you are touch my life so deeply that I can live my life assured of my identity in you. In your name I pray. Amen.

# 5

# The likeness of the invisible God

Paul, an apostle of Christ Jesus by the will of God, and Timothy our brother . . . He is the image of the invisible God, the firstborn of all creation; for in him all things in heaven and on earth were created, things visible and invisible, whether thrones or dominions or rulers or powers – all things have been created through him and for him. He himself is before all things, and in him all things hold together. He is the head of the body, the church; he is the beginning, the firstborn from the dead, so that he might come to have first place in everything. For in him all the fullness of God was pleased to dwell, and through him God was pleased to reconcile to himself all things, whether on earth or in heaven, by making peace through the blood of his cross.

(Col. 1.1, 15–20)

Picture a pebble hitting the still surface of a lake. Mark Oakley in his book *The Splash of Words* explains how reading a poem can have a similar kind of disrupting effect on us: even after the initial 'splash' effect, there are ripples. These ripples of meaning continue to transform us and our understanding.[1]

This wonderful poem in Colossians has always had this effect on me. It uses striking and evocative language to publicly declare the complete sufficiency of God's revelation and salvation in Jesus Christ. He is on the throne, with pre-eminence over all powers.

We are engulfed in images of Jesus Christ. He is the first-born; he is the head; he is the beginning; he has first place in everything; but, most importantly, he is the image of God. In antiquity the 'image' (Greek *eikon*) of a ruler was his picture on a coin. The coin made the ruler visible and 'omnipresent' among his subjects. It stood for the ruler. That is what is being said about Jesus Christ. He bears the very stamp of God, the image or likeness of the divine. We see Jesus Christ and we know something about God.

Paul wants to emphasize the 'fullness' (*pleroma*) of this revelation. This is not an inferior copy of God or a temporary stand-in for God. He writes, 'For in him all the fullness of God was pleased to dwell', (Col 1.19; see also 2.9). It is 'in the face of Jesus Christ' that we can know God (2 Cor. 4.6). During Jesus' earthly ministry, Philip asked him, 'Lord, show us the Father, and we will be satisfied.' Jesus responded, 'Have I been with you all this time, Philip, and you still do not know me? Whoever has seen me has seen the Father. How can you say, "Show us the Father"?' (John 14.8–9). The wonderful truth is that the more we look at Jesus the more we can see God, the true God of utter self-giving love.

Hebrews 1.3 puts it powerfully when it speaks of the Son as 'the reflection of God's glory and the exact imprint of God's very being'. Christ is the radiance of God. We can think of the 'reflection' of God's glory like the sun. The sun shines its light. And, just as the radiance of the sun reaches out from itself to give light and warmth to the world, so Jesus Christ is the radiance of God, which brings God from a cosmic location to our individual hearts. The brightness of the sun has the same nature as the sun: it is as old as the sun, and the sun has never been without its brightness. Its brightness can't be separated from the sun, yet it is not the sun. So Jesus Christ is God, the express image of his person – the exact reproduction of God, the image of God, the equal of God. We may have many questions about God, but we do not need to fumble in the dark when it comes to knowing what God is like. To call Jesus the *eikon* of God is to say that he is the perfect portrait.

The ripple effects of this passage are huge. I would encourage you to read and re-read it, allowing the words to transform you and your understanding.

## Action

Read and re-read Colossians 1.15–20. Allow this poem to have its ripple effect in you.

## Prayer

Almighty God,
who sent your Holy Spirit
to be the life and light of your Church:
open our hearts to the riches of your grace,
that we may bring forth the fruit of the Spirit
in love and joy and peace;
through Jesus Christ your Son, our Lord,
who is alive and reigns with you,

in the unity of the Holy Spirit,
one God, now and for ever.
Amen.
(Collect for the Ninth Sunday after Trinity, *Common Worship*)

## Note

1 Mark Oakley, *The Splash of Words* (Norwich: Canterbury Press, 2016), p. xv.

# 6

# The reflection of God's glory

Long ago God spoke to our ancestors in many and
various ways by the prophets, but in these last days
he has spoken to us by a Son, whom he appointed
heir of all things, through whom he also created the
world. He is the reflection of God's glory and the exact
imprint of God's very being, and he sustains all things
by his powerful word. When he had made purification
for sins, he sat down at the right hand of the Majesty
on high, having become as much superior to angels
as the name he has inherited is more excellent than
theirs.
(Heb. 1.1–4)

We have got used to hype in the worlds of advertising, politics and commerce – it's all around us. In 1920s USA, the
emergence of Wonder Bread, which for the first time came
ready sliced, led to a slogan that is now a term of affectionate
mockery – 'the best thing since sliced bread'.

The dispersed Jewish Christians who received the letter
to the Hebrews seem to have needed a reminder that Jesus
wasn't just the best thing since sliced bread, but he was undoubtedly the Messiah, superior to the angels, to Moses and
to the Levitical priesthood. Indeed, he established a new
covenant between God and humanity.

Hebrews chapter 1 insists that we have a God who reveals himself, who speaks – through Scripture and through the prophets – but whose final Word is Jesus Christ. Seven assertions are made about Jesus:

- He is the heir of all things (v. 2): when this universe is wound up, he will be at the end-point to inherit the new heavens and the new earth.
- He is the author of creation (v. 2): as the world evolved, Christ was there and spoke things into existence.
- He is the radiance of God (v. 3) – the word is 'effulgence': Christ shines into the world with the light of God, illuminating all things.
- He is the image of God (v. 3): if you want to know what God is like, look at Jesus Christ, God incarnate.
- He is the sustainer of all things (v. 3): Christians understand God to be intimately involved with the continuing life of the world.
- He is the one who bore our sins (v. 3): the mystery of his death on the cross has made forgiveness and new life available to us.
- He is the one who has completed the work of salvation (v. 3), having now ascended to the Father.

I came to Christianity from atheism, and it was an encounter with Jesus Christ and his love that brought me to the Christian faith. Whenever I doubt the reality of God, it is Jesus Christ to whom I am drawn back again and again – his life, death, resurrection and invitation to live in his story. The letters in the New Testament were written to encourage

Christians that the teaching they had embraced grounds itself in a trustworthy picture of the one they had come to follow. The Christian story is shown to us to be the only true story – the one that matters. To paraphrase C. S. Lewis, our faith is like the sun in the sky. We not only see its light as we observe the world, but by that light we see the rest of reality as well.[1]

Hebrews encourages us towards this radical understanding of the Christian faith. If all this were true, there is nowhere else to go. Readers of the letter are invited to make a clear response – to run the race looking to Jesus (Heb. 12.1–2). I remember doing the Couch to 5K running programme. The first weeks were torture – my lungs, legs and mind were all struggling. It wasn't until about the sixth week, when my stamina and mindset had adjusted to the new discipline, that my body began to accept that running 5K was going to be possible. But I had to embrace it wholeheartedly in order to get there. Running the race as Hebrews describes it is to accept that once you have come, by faith, to live the Christian story, you have no other option. You have to run, with your eyes fixed on Jesus Christ.

## Action

What do you need to hear from God about the character and nature of the Jesus whom we follow? Read through the seven facets of the work of Jesus from Hebrews chapter 1 and give thanks to God for them. Which of those will you take into your day?

## Prayer

We give you thanks and praise, Father in heaven,
through Jesus Christ, your only Son, our Lord.
Through him you created the world.
Through his word the universe is sustained.
Through him you completed the work of our
    salvation.
Give us grace to run with him through our life in
    the world today. Amen.

## Note

1 See C. S. Lewis, 'Is Theology Poetry?', in *The Weight of Glory and Other Addresses* (Grand Rapids, MI: Zondervan, 2001), p. 141.

# 7

# He revealed his glory

On the third day there was a wedding in Cana of Galilee, and the mother of Jesus was there. Jesus and his disciples had also been invited to the wedding. When the wine gave out, the mother of Jesus said to him, 'They have no wine.' And Jesus said to her, 'Woman, what concern is that to you and to me? My hour has not yet come.' His mother said to the servants, 'Do whatever he tells you.' Now standing there were six stone water-jars for the Jewish rites of purification, each holding twenty or thirty gallons. Jesus said to them, 'Fill the jars with water.' And they filled them up to the brim. He said to them, 'Now draw some out, and take it to the chief steward.' So they took it. When the steward tasted the water that had become wine, and did not know where it came from (though the servants who had drawn the water knew), the steward called the bridegroom and said to him, 'Everyone serves the good wine first, and then the inferior wine after the guests have become drunk. But you have kept the good wine until now.' Jesus did this, the first of his signs, in Cana of Galilee, and revealed his glory; and his disciples believed in him.

After this he went down to Capernaum with his mother, his brothers, and his disciples; and they remained there for a few days.
(John 2.1–12)

Often, at the beginning of the wedding service, the priest will remind the congregation of words from St John's first letter that 'God is love, and those who abide in love abide in God, and God abides in them' (1 John 4.16). This is an extraordinary statement, which reinforces God's desire to be in a relationship with each one of us, such is his wonderful generosity.

These words are especially powerful, when, quite often, the journey to get to the wedding day has been fraught with all sorts of emotions and tensions. Wedding planning is an intense business, and the image, the story and the culture, as expressions of our own complexities, can be hard to navigate, with the pressure that the day should be 'perfect'. Trying to meet the expectations of Great-Aunt Agatha, or Uncle Dennis, whom we see only at Christmas, alongside those of Dave or Judy, whom we see every week down the pub, can be very difficult. The arrangements for table seating alone can be a minefield.

Weddings bring out the best and the worst in people, and this can sometimes be revealed at the wedding rehearsal. Both wedding rehearsals and weddings remind us of real life because they speak of creative and fragile human beings, who have decided to become vulnerable and share their lives with one another, in the same way that Jesus became vulnerable by sharing his life with us through his incarnation.

It is not surprising, then, that St John chooses to tell the miraculous story of Jesus at a wedding near the beginning of his Gospel, an occasion that is full of expectation and hope for two families and for the wider community. This wedding would have lasted for several days and would have said much about the image of themselves that the families involved wanted to convey. The whole community would have been invited as a symbol of both generosity and perhaps status. It would have been a boozy affair, and the organizers' reputation would have been at stake.

Just imagine the complete humiliation when the wine then ran out. This was a disaster. The families would have been so embarrassed. This was one of the worst things that could have happened. But, behind the scenes, Jesus, as he so often does, is rebuilding relationships and meeting with people in their places of deepest vulnerability. With Mary's instruction to 'Do whatever he tells you', the stage has been set for this first miracle.

There in the room was water in stone jars. This water was for washing the feet of visitors, as a sign of hospitality, welcome and status. Jesus quietly decides to take this water and transform it into wine. The chief steward, whose job would have been on the line after the wine ran out, is given some of the water from the stone jars to taste. He is astounded and calls the bridegroom over to ask about this wonderful new wine. The bridegroom's humiliation has now been averted, and you can sense his enormous relief.

This image of Jesus transforming water into wine is remarkable. Jesus meets with individuals in their humiliation and vulnerability, and quietly works behind the scenes.

Mary's prophetic words of following God's word in Jesus paves the way for this. There was an expectation, among the many competing expectations on that day, that Jesus would act, be present and change the culture by responding to people's vulnerability. All the ingredients for this simple miracle were in the room. Nothing was brought in, but the water and the jars were given a new purpose: they were seen differently and they glorified God in new ways, having been blessed by Jesus.

## Action

Perhaps this Lent we need to look at ourselves and our motives. How do we meet others in their vulnerability or force our expectations on others? Perhaps we should also look around us? Who has skills and gifts that have not yet been discovered, and how might such skills and gifts be used differently in our households, workplaces and churches? All that was needed for this miracle was already in the room. But it needed to be discovered. What will today hold if you were to 'do whatever he tells you'?

## Prayer

Dear Lord, help me to see you at work. Normally, when I am vulnerable I only look inwards to my own insecurities. Help me to look outwards and to see all that you have given to me as gifts, and to help me also to look to you, for you are with me in all things. Amen.

# 8

# Taken up into glory

Glory be to the Father, and to the Son, and to the Holy Spirit: as it was in the beginning, is now and ever shall be, world without end. Amen.

This conclusion to the recitation of a psalm or psalms in the liturgical worship of the Church, at Morning or Evening Prayer for example, is familiar to us. The formula is known as the doxology, and the English term derives partly from the Greek *doxa*, which means 'glory'. *Doxa* is the last word in Greek in the passage which gives us the text for this meditation, from the third chapter of the first letter of St Paul to Timothy (3.16):

He was revealed in flesh,
    vindicated in spirit,
        seen by angels,
proclaimed among Gentiles,
    believed in throughout the world,
        taken up in glory.

The 'he' at the beginning of this passage is, of course, Jesus Christ, and most commentators agree that the author of 1 Timothy – St Paul or someone very close to him – is here quoting a very early Christian hymn, or profession of faith, which encompasses all the principal mysteries of the incarnate life of Christ: his coming as a man ('revealed in flesh'), his resurrection ('vindicated'), his adoration in heaven ('seen by angels'), his spread of the gospel ('proclaimed . . . believed') and his ascension ('taken up in glory').

We may find it surprising that doctrine (which we tend to think of as dry and unpromising) should provide the material for a scriptural hymn of praise. But doctrine simply means that which is taught, and what the early Church taught, received and handed on about Jesus is essential to our understanding of why his birth, death and resurrection constitute good news for the whole human race, and indeed for the entire universe. Had Jesus not been truly God incarnate – the Word made flesh – there would be no salvation. Had Jesus died on the cross and not risen, there would be no salvation. Had the message of Jesus crucified and risen not been taken to the ends of the earth, there would be no salvation. Had Jesus not returned into the heavens in his humanity as in his divinity, there would be no salvation. You understand the point!

The Catholic poet, essayist, epigrammatist and wit Hilaire Belloc (1870–1953) admonished his readers not to 'monkey with the Creed'.[1]

The first letter to Timothy was, of course, composed long before the Church came to define her faith in the words of the creeds which we still recite at the celebration of the Eucharist on Sundays and holy days. But in this passage from the New Testament, we see the outlines of the key beliefs about Jesus that Christians proclaim. Doctrine matters. Teaching the faith matters. This is why we must pray for bishops, whose calling is to guard the faith of the Church, and for theologians, whose vocation is to explore, test and expound that faith in new contexts in every age. Studying the Scriptures and the Christian tradition matters, so that we may become ever more committed and faithful disciples.

Remember the Greek word *doxa*, 'glory'. Praise gives glory to God, and praise flows from our apprehension of who God is and what he has done for us, supremely in taking flesh for our sake in Jesus Christ, and in Christ suffering, dying and rising again for us. The more we apprehend the truths of the Christian faith – what the author of 1 Timothy calls 'the mystery of our religion' (3.16) – the more we shall find ourselves wanting to praise God as we come to understand (however falteringly) the wonderful things he has done for us.

## Action

Spend some time reflecting slowly, prayerfully, on the words of the Nicene Creed, pausing after each clause and giving thanks to God for what these words reveal to you.

## Prayer

A prayer of St Anselm (Archbishop of Canterbury, 1093–1109) from his *Proslogion*:

I am not trying to attain to your heights, O Lord, by no means can my understanding compare with that. Yet I still want, in some measure, to understand your truth, which my heart believes and loves. Nor am I trying to understand in order to believe, rather I believe in order to understand. Moreover, I believe that, unless I believed, I would not understand.[2]

## Notes

1 From one of his *Cautionary Tales for Children*, quoted by Robert Royal, *A Deeper Vision* (San Francisco, CA: Ignatius Press, 2015), p. 384.
2 Translated by the author.

Part 2

# OUR CALLING
# AND BAPTISM

# 9

# Follow me

As he walked by the Sea of Galilee, he saw two brothers,
Simon, who is called Peter, and Andrew his brother,
casting a net into the lake – for they were fishermen.
And he said to them, 'Follow me, and I will make you
fish for people.' Immediately they left their nets and
followed him. As he went from there, he saw two other
brothers, James son of Zebedee and his brother John,
in the boat with their father Zebedee, mending their
nets, and he called them. Immediately they left the boat
and their father, and followed him.
(Matt. 4.18–22)

I was brought up a Christian, and my faith became in-
creasingly important to me in my mid-teens. Church fed
the mystic dreamer in me, the teenager who was captivated
by literature, old buildings and tradition, by the lives of
the northern saints and their travels in faith out along the
northern coast. Church also fed the intellectual butterfly
in me, the teenager who was longing to emerge from the
cocoon of 1980s suburban Teesside. I found church to be
a place that broadened my horizons spiritually, intellectu-
ally, and socially, and that gave me a thirst for travel and
learning. This didn't initially lead me towards ministry –
vocations for women were not talked about or seen in any

churches I attended. Instead, it led me towards graduate and postgraduate study at home and abroad.

It dearly mattered to me that I was going to be an academic. I desperately wanted to belong somewhere that seemed culturally not only out of my reach but even sometimes disdainful of students from non-traditional backgrounds like mine. As the first person in my family to go to university, and aware of some of the dissonance that cultural alienation brought, I decided that if I was going to do this I was going straight for the jackpot. I completed a doctorate, was just about to start my first year as a lecturer in English at an Oxford college and was feeling pleased about the possibilities that were opening up, when a trip to deliver a conference paper took me via New York.

New York was vibrant and fizzing with energy in a warm late September 1997. It felt edgy and dangerous, more diverse and fast-paced than anything I was used to. I marvelled at people who walked past me with characteristic New York style and confidence. While enlivened by the city's buzz, I also felt lost and lonely.

Seeking sanctuary from the lively pavements, I stumbled into a large church and knelt to pray. The stillness descended and, as my eyes adjusted to the cool shade, I began to pick out the familiar sights: pulpit, cross, altar. I can't quite describe what happened next, but I was acutely aware, to the point of being moved to tears, of God's presence with me, and of a voice that told me to follow him. I knew at that point that I was being called into a new future, which would involve laying down what I had previously worshipped. It would mean setting aside the affirmation I drew from academic achievement and starting again, empty-handed, trying to discern what kind of ministry God might be calling me to.

I had been a Christian previously, but the idea that following Jesus would make such a radical difference to my life was new. So too was a sense of giving control of my life to God rather than carefully plotting out a career for myself. I also needed to admit that I had been wrong about what I had thought my path in life would be – and being a highly defensive person, I was not good at admitting that I was wrong about anything. Some of my tears were of joy, and some were of loss.

When we say yes to Jesus, our lives change. Jesus' first call to everyone is to repent, for the kingdom of heaven has come near. And then in Matthew's Gospel comes the double calling of the first disciples – first, Simon Peter and Andrew, then James and John – who are asked to lay down their professions – not only to hear the word of God but to act on it.

Becoming a disciple of Christ involves a profound life change, saying yes to God and committing oneself to follow Jesus. I admire those four first disciples for so immediately laying down their fishing nets, leaving their boat and even leaving Zebedee, the father of two of them. I am still learning to lay down my life and to filter out the ever-present clamour of the world – to hear the voice of Jesus and to follow him alone.

## Action

Find a place of stillness – by the sea, in the woods or in an urban sanctuary – and take time to listen for the voice of

Jesus. Ask yourself what you are being called to lay down. Where is God leading you? How is Jesus showing you how to fish for people?

## Prayer

Lord, I am good at mending nets; let me continue
    my work.
Lord, I can make a fine day's wages fishing; let me
    feed my family.
Lord, there are people who depend on me, people
    who are expecting me home shortly;
don't make me let them down.
Jesus, I hear your voice; I don't know what you are
    asking.
Jesus, your voice is churning me up; it is calling me
    not only to listen but to change.
Jesus, I am willing, but you need to show me the
    way.
Spirit, take my feet and plant them in Jesus'
    footsteps.
Spirit, give me words to speak what burns in my
    heart.
Spirit, breathe your life within me and together we
    will fish for people.
Amen.

# 10

# Come and see

The next day John again was standing with two of his disciples, and as he watched Jesus walk by, he exclaimed, 'Look, here is the Lamb of God!' The two disciples heard him say this, and they followed Jesus. When Jesus turned and saw them following, he said to them, 'What are you looking for?' They said to him, 'Rabbi' (which translated means Teacher), 'where are you staying?' He said to them, 'Come and see.' They came and saw where he was staying, and they remained with him that day. It was about four o'clock in the afternoon. One of the two who heard John speak and followed him was Andrew, Simon Peter's brother. He first found his brother Simon and said to him, 'We have found the Messiah' (which is translated Anointed). He brought Simon to Jesus, who looked at him and said, 'You are Simon son of John. You are to be called Cephas' (which is translated Peter).
(John 1.35–42)

What first drew you into the Christian faith? Maybe you grew up in the Church. Maybe you came to faith through the ministry of a priest at a time of bereavement or when you had your baby christened. Perhaps you went on an Alpha or a Pilgrim course. Maybe you met God on your own. When I officiate at confirmation services, I love hearing the stories of the candidates' journeys to faith – rich, diverse, stimulating. The common theme is that of a journey of discovery – finding Jesus Christ and becoming his followers, fascinated by who he is.

St John's story of the calling of the first disciples is crafted carefully. The beginning of his Gospel is narrated in terms of 'days' ('the next day . . . the next day'). He's not being chronological – rather, he's indicating the progression of Jesus' ministry, and the way in which John the Baptist signposts him as the Messiah. The Baptist declares Jesus to be the Lamb of God (v. 36) (he's already introduced that phrase in the previous section, in v. 29). This is Messiah language, channelling Isaiah's prophecies, Abraham's sacrificial lamb and apocalyptic promises. 'Behold, the Lamb of God' would immediately get the interest of those who were looking for the Coming One. John the Baptist's disciples are intrigued.

The question Jesus poses – for them and for us – is 'What are you looking for?' Intellectual curiosity is often a starting point in the quest for faith. Jesus invites them to come and see; they acclaim him as a rabbi; they join him where he is staying. We discover that one of these disciples of the Baptist is actually Andrew, who in turn invites his brother Simon Peter along.

The intellectual quest can take us only so far. Jesus presumably began to answer their questions about what it might mean for him to be the Messiah, but they are still on the journey. It falls to Philip and Nathanael in the next section of the Gospel to make a slighter deeper response – though still at this stage pretty superficial ('I saw you under the fig tree', v. 48). It's going to take a lot more journeying, listening and watching Jesus before these men truly embrace discipleship. But that's OK – Jesus takes us as we are, not in some idealized world of spiritual coherence. When we get to the place where we can say, with Andrew, 'We have found the Messiah' (v. 41) – that's when the journey really starts to take off.

John's Gospel will take the disciples on that journey – moving from interest and intellectual curiosity to seven signs that point to Jesus as he really is – changing water into wine, healing, feeding the 5,000 and finally (and perhaps what makes his arrest and death inevitable) raising Lazarus from the dead. The disciples, for their part, will be provoked to faith, challenged to discipleship and invited to a new relationship based on love. They don't become the finished article in the Gospel narrative – Thomas doubts, Peter denies and Judas betrays Jesus. In our lives, too, our following of Jesus is not straightforward. We'll mess up and be unfaithful just like the first disciples. But the good news is that he holds on to us. God is faithful even when we are faithless. He doesn't let go. Lent reminds us that, when we fall short, confession, forgiveness and restoration can enable us to continue the journey.

## Action

Reflect on where you are in your journey with Jesus. When you found yourself invited to 'Come and see', what happened next? What would you like to happen next in your Christian journey? What might you want to say to God, to your church friends, to your priest about the 'what next'?

## Prayer

Almighty God,
who gave such grace to your apostle Saint Andrew
that he readily obeyed the call of your Son Jesus
    Christ and brought his brother with him:
call us by your holy word,
and give us grace to follow you without delay
and to tell the good news of your kingdom;
through Jesus Christ your Son our Lord. Amen.
(Collect for St Andrew's Day, *Common Worship*)

# 11

# Buried with him in baptism

What then are we to say? Should we continue in sin in order that grace may abound? By no means! How can we who died to sin go on living in it? Do you not know that all of us who have been baptized into Christ Jesus were baptized into his death? Therefore we have been buried with him by baptism into death, so that, just as Christ was raised from the dead by the glory of the Father, so we too might walk in newness of life.

For if we have been united with him in a death like his, we will certainly be united with him in a resurrection like his. We know that our old self was crucified with him so that the body of sin might be destroyed, and we might no longer be enslaved to sin. For whoever has died is freed from sin. But if we have died with Christ, we believe that we will also live with him. We know that Christ, being raised from the dead, will never die again; death no longer has dominion over him. The death he died, he died to sin, once for all; but the life he lives, he lives to God. So you also must consider yourselves dead to sin and alive to God in Christ Jesus.
(Rom. 6.1–11)

From time to time, glossy Sunday supplements or lifestyle magazines run articles offering radical personal change. You can find online a diet plan called 'New You', a hardcore fitness boot camp with the same name and a similarly entitled cosmetic surgery practice promising 'nose re-shaping', double chin remodelling and the removal of excess stomach fat.

In this passage in Romans, St Paul uses a similar image to describe what happens when a person becomes a follower of Christ. Baptism is a kind of death of the old self and the rising of a new one, a 'new you' as it were, not through a new diet but through dying and rising with Christ. Just as Christ died, his body bruised, battered and nailed to a cross, and then rose again, still the same person but with a transfigured and transformed body, we too descend into the waters of death with him, and as we come up again, dripping wet, we rise again with him, still the same person yet radically different.

St Paul writes here of our 'old self' and in Ephesians 4.24, of our 'new self, created according to the likeness of God'. That old self is the one defined by our mistakes, failures, or wins and achievements. It may be the old self that always seeks to be the centre of attention, that gets irritated if people don't recognize our worth, that wants to get its own way. That old self was 'crucified with Christ' (Gal. 2.19). It is as if the old you or me died at the moment of baptism, left behind in the waters of death as we rose to a new life and a new identity with Christ.

Sometimes, people who have witnessed a crime, or juvenile offenders who are released from prison to try to start their lives again, can no longer stay as they are. They may be the target of old enemies or people with a lasting grudge. Such people are sometimes given new identities – a new name, address, passport, clothes and the rest. Living with a new identity is not easy. A consultant forensic psychiatrist, asked about the difficulty such people experience, said: 'Double lives are a burden for people. Just juggling two relationships is stressful and the secrecy takes its toll. People are not necessarily well equipped to do this sort of thing; it's not their natural state.'[1] It's not easy living out a new identity, trying to live a new life while the old one still lurks around. Such people often feel a compulsion to go back and to live their old existence secretly, living out of who they once were, not who they are now freed to be.

It's a picture of what St Paul meant in this image. To follow the way of Jesus is to learn to leave behind that old self, the one wrapped up in itself, forever anxious about the judgement of other people. It is to welcome a new self, 'created in Christ Jesus for good works, which God prepared beforehand to be our way of life' (Eph. 2.10).

Baptism is not just an occasion for a family party after a baby's birth or a gentle lifestyle option for the aimless. The theologian Michael Jinkins writes:

Baptism is a word for dying, a word for shipwreck. In Hellenistic Greek, it meant death. We are soaked to the skin in the death of Christ. Our union with Christ drips from us. We never 'get over' this immersion; this drowning in Christ's death marks us daily. It marks us out, 'names' us to the world and to one another as 'children of God'. We are shipwrecked, run aground on the death of Christ; we trail wet footprints of this drenching wherever we go; we never dry off.[2]

## Action

Baptism marks us out as new people. Our task today is to live out of that new identity, not the old one, looking out for the Christ-like actions and gestures that we can make towards others and the world around us.

## Prayer

We thank you, our Father, for the new start we were given in our baptism into Christ. Help us to live as new people today, stepping into and embracing the good works you have prepared for us in Christ. Amen.

## Notes

1 Quoted by Jamie Doward, 'James Bulger killer Jon Venables confessed real identity to strangers as mental state crumbled', *The Guardian*, 7 March 2010, <https://www.theguardian.com/uk/2010/mar/07/jon-venables-confessed-identity>.

2 Michael Jinkins, *The Church Faces Death: Ecclesiology in a post-modern context* (New York: Oxford University Press, 1999), p. 23.

# 12

# Those who call on the name of the Lord

Moses writes concerning the righteousness that comes from the law, that 'the person who does these things will live by them'. But the righteousness that comes from faith says, 'Do not say in your heart, "Who will ascend into heaven?"' (that is, to bring Christ down) 'or "Who will descend into the abyss?"' (that is, to bring Christ up from the dead). But what does it say?

'The word is near you,

on your lips and in your heart'

(that is, the word of faith that we proclaim); because if you confess with your lips that Jesus is Lord and believe in your heart that God raised him from the dead, you will be saved. For one believes with the heart and so is justified, and one confesses with the mouth and so is saved. The Scripture says, 'No one who believes in him will be put to shame.' For there is no distinction between Jew and Greek; the same Lord is Lord of all and is generous to all who call on him. For, 'Everyone who calls on the name of the Lord shall be saved.' (Rom. 10.5–13)

Devotees of the Harry Potter books will know of the power that is given to the name of Voldemort, the dark wizard. People were afraid to say his name aloud. In the last book of the series, a taboo is attached to the name, so that anyone who uttered it could be detected wherever they were. We recognize the power of names and what they represent.

St Paul's letter to the Christians in Rome is a sustained explanation of the good news of Jesus Christ which answers the questions 'What is the gospel?', 'Why do we need it?', 'Can we be saved by keeping the law?', 'What does it mean to have faith?', 'How does Jesus' death and resurrection put us right with God?' By the time he reaches chapter 10, Paul wants to assert the universality of the good news – that salvation is for all. To call upon the name of Jesus, he argues, is to be saved – the polar opposite of the oppressive and evil name of Voldemort: 'Everyone who calls upon the name of the Lord shall be saved' (v. 13).

This is a very different power in a name! In chapter 9, Paul completed his demolition of the idea that keeping the law can bring salvation – Israel, who has relied on the law, will come to salvation only through faith, as will the whole world. Indeed, it is ludicrous to suggest that a person can be saved by keeping the law. You may just as well try to clamber up to heaven to find the ascended Christ (v. 6), or to go down to the abyss to bring Christ up from the dead (v. 7). Salvation is much simpler than meaningless quests to search for Jesus Christ, for he is accessible to all by faith (v. 8).

In a pub conversation one of my friends who is not (yet) a Christian raised the objection, 'Your trouble is that you want to make it too easy to have faith.' The life of discipleship is not, of course, an easy option, but there *is* simplicity in the first step of the journey. Paul quotes the Old Testament (Deut. 30.14) – 'The word is near you, on your lips and in your heart' – to link together the necessity for inward belief and outward profession. There's no such thing as a secret Christian: 'if you confess with your lips that Jesus is Lord and believe in your heart that God raised him from the dead, you will be saved' (v. 9).

When I first found faith, I was a bit reticent. I'd been an atheist up till then and didn't really want to tell the world about my change of heart – it felt like a major climb-down from the public stance I'd previously taken. But my cover was blown by my youth leader, who told my mates that I'd become a Christian. I had the inward belief that Jesus was risen from the dead, but I needed to make an outward profession, which I then gladly did, and was later baptized as a further visible sign of faith. The power of profession became, for the early Church, a simple antecedent of the Creed – 'Jesus is Lord.'

The effect of this inward and outward confession is that it roots the gospel in our lives: we believe internally, and are justified (put right with God); we confess with our mouth externally and receive by grace God's gift of salvation (v. 10). The power of the name is transformational.

## Action

Are there contexts where you find it difficult to be explicit about your faith? Are you tempted to be an anonymous believer, but know that you need to break cover and confess the faith? Is the Holy Spirit nudging you to be baptized or confirmed? What is the next step in your faith journey?

## Prayer

Spirit of truth, lead us into all truth,
Give us grace to confess that Jesus Christ is Lord,
and to proclaim the word and works of God. Amen.
(Adapted from Seasonal Blessings, *Common Worship*)

# 13

# Given us new birth

Blessed be the God and Father of our Lord Jesus Christ!
By his great mercy he has given us a new birth into a
living hope through the resurrection of Jesus Christ from
the dead, and into an inheritance that is imperishable,
undefiled, and unfading, kept in heaven for you, who are
being protected by the power of God through faith for
a salvation ready to be revealed in the last time.
(1 Pet. 1.3–5)

Nicodemus, a Pharisee and a leader of the Jews, came to
Jesus at night for a secret, private meeting, away from the
crowds that hovered around him during the day (John 3.1–
12). He was on a journey just like us, passing from darkness
into light. He asked:

'Rabbi, we know that you are a teacher who has come
from God; for no one can do these signs that you do
apart from the presence of God.' Jesus answered him,
'Very truly, I tell you, no one can see the kingdom of
God without being born from above.'
(John 3.2–3)

Jesus, a master of wordplay, often used words and images
that were not always meant to be taken literally. The words

that have been translated as 'born from above' (or 'born anew') would have left the original readers as bemused as Nicodemus. What do they mean?

Some years after Nicodemus' secret rendezvous, Peter focuses on one implication, as he writes to encourage scattered Christians in what is now modern-day Turkey. He explains that this new birth moves us from despair to hope, a secure hope of new citizenship now and of an inheritance to come that is imperishable and undefiled.

This hope is a gift through God's great mercy. Because we have been sprinkled by Christ's blood on the cross (1 Pet. 1.2), those things that would have separated us from God no longer do. Our sins are washed away. We are born, as Jesus put it to Nicodemus, 'of water', a washing that is symbolized in baptism, by the power of the Holy Spirit (John 3.6).

It is important to stress that the hope into which we enter is not blind optimism. It is not based on wishful thinking or fantasy. It is about a knowledge of the future, secured by the resurrection (1 Pet. 1.4), which leaps into our present. And it does so in such a way that we feel secure in the here and now.

This future is one in which God's kingdom is fully realized, an eternal life in which there is no more death and dying. This hope is stored up for us in heaven and, while it may break into our present, it is something that we wait patiently to see in full.

The promise of new birth also means being part of a new family and therefore enjoying a new citizenship, which bestows greater benefits than anything the world can offer and which is not bound by our present hopes or troubles.

We are told by the author of Hebrews that hope is an anchor for the soul, firm and secure. It is that which holds us when we are living in the shadow of suffering and death. When I was the Canon Treasurer at Salisbury Cathedral my purple cope had an anchor on the back. I often commented that it was not as interesting as the symbols that my colleagues displayed. They had chalices, crosses and stars. But it is the anchor that is seen in the east end of the cathedral in the striking blue Prisoners of Conscience window. It reminds us that it is hope that is the anchor of our soul, which holds us when we find our lives interwoven with the struggle between life and death, darkness and light. It is hope that holds us in the face of the death and suffering in our own lives.

New birth through the resurrection of Jesus Christ offers an unshakeable hope. The possibility of new beginnings and transformation not just for the individual but also for communities of people who follow Jesus Christ.

## Action

Look out for new life around you today – whether it be spring bloom or the birth of children. Use that as an opportunity to give thanks for the hope that our new birth secures.

## Prayer

Almighty God,
give us such a vision of your purpose
and such an assurance of your love and power,
that we may ever hold fast the hope

which is in Jesus Christ our Lord,
who is alive with you and the Holy Spirit,
one God now and for ever.
Amen.

# 14

# All one in Christ Jesus

As many of you as were baptized into Christ have clothed yourselves with Christ. There is no longer Jew or Greek, there is no longer slave or free, there is no longer male and female; for all of you are one in Christ Jesus.

(Gal. 3.27–28)

One of my favourite children's books, read often to our youngest with squeals of delight at the predictably unpredictable ending, is Mem Fox's *Ten Little Fingers and Ten Little Toes*.[1] It describes two infants, one born in distant lands, and another the following day. The babies have similarities and differences, but their key similarity, as the book illustrates, is that both babies have ten little fingers and ten little toes. The story continues, describing babies in towns, wrapped in blankets, living in tents, surviving wintry climates, babies lovable and babies loved. Each of them, as every listener soon knows, has ten little fingers and ten little toes.

And just as the repeated rhythmic patterns are building securely in the listeners' heads, and as a final double couplet appears to bring the story home to rest, the narrator catches us unawares, adding in an extra phrase. The final baby in the picture book doesn't just have ten fingers and ten toes . . . it also has several kisses on the end of its nose.

Cue kisses, and squeals of delight. Every time.

Beautifully illustrated by Helen Oxenbury, the book is brought to life with pictures of babies from across the world; born into many different situations, they have different skin colour, clothing and companions. Yet, as the refrain reminds us, all the babies are more similar than they are different, with their ten little fingers and ten little toes.

As we grow in the Christian faith, whether born into it as children or through the leading of the Spirit later in life, we receive treasured accounts of where we have come from and where we now belong. The stories of our ancestors in faith, the teachings of Jesus and the earliest Christians' first understandings of the meaning of Christ's life, death and resurrection, all shape our sense of identity.

In Galatians, Paul brings his own beliefs home to rest as he shows how each of us is God's adopted child and heir. He teaches that we are all one in Jesus Christ, with no distinctions because of our background, status or gender. Our adoption brings us into direct relationship with a loving God, a relationship which is tender and intimate, as we see Jesus himself demonstrating in conversations with his heavenly Father.

We can easily be encouraged by the world to lose sight of our fundamental equality in God, both because injustice and racism are tolerated and because our self-esteem can become so dented by worldly experience that we find it hard to believe God truly loves us. But despite the sin that cuts off some lives at the root, what Paul is telling us about how God sees us is still true. We are all God's children, and God loves us and promises to be with us on our journey through life.

Whether or not we are parents, it is not difficult to imagine reading with love and tenderness to a child and assuring them that to those who love them and to God they are special and beloved children. What is harder, especially if we have not known secure, loving parenting in our own lives, is to believe that this applies to us too.

It does. We are God's beloved children: with the Spirit in our hearts, we belong to him in Christ.

## Action

Read a children's book – one you have at home, or find in a library or browse (and hopefully buy) in a bookshop. What can you learn about God from it? Dwell in the knowledge that God is present with you from birth to the end of time and feel God gazing on you now in love.

## Prayer

Whether we are born near or far away,
whether we have plenty or experience want,
we are all one in Christ Jesus.
Free us from prejudice
and from self-doubt,
that we might clothe ourselves in Christ
and know that we are God's beloved children.
Amen.

## Note

1 Mem Fox, *Ten Little Fingers and Ten Little Toes*, illus. Helen Oxenbury (London: Walker, 2008).

# 15

# Go and make disciples

Now the eleven disciples went to Galilee, to the mountain to which Jesus had directed them. When they saw him, they worshipped him; but some doubted. And Jesus came and said to them, 'All authority in heaven and on earth has been given to me. Go therefore and make disciples of all nations, baptizing them in the name of the Father and of the Son and of the Holy Spirit, and teaching them to obey everything that I have commanded you. And remember, I am with you always, to the end of the age.'
(Matt. 28.16–20)

The call to follow Jesus is a call not just for us alone. As he calls us, he sends us to help others to follow him too. If you think about it, someone helped you to follow Christ – whether it was your parents, a relative or a friend, or perhaps as you read the Bible for yourself. And what we have received, we are encouraged to pass on to others.

The last words of Jesus that Matthew records in his Gospel are a commission to his disciples. A commission is an instruction, command or role given to a person or a group. But this commission is one that is a recommission in each generation because Jesus says, '[teach] them to obey everything that I have commanded you'. It is in essence a multiplying commission. We are the recipients of this commission and we in turn are commissioned to play our part in it too. Jesus tells the disciples to:

- 'Go': we are not to hold back our faith from others but to go to those around us, anywhere that God leads us.
- 'Make disciples': we are not just to *be* disciples ourselves, but we are encouraged by Jesus to *make* disciples. That means asking ourselves the question 'Who can I disciple?' It may mean helping someone in the Church to grow as a disciple. Or it may mean helping someone who is not yet a Christian to come to know Jesus for themselves. The disciples spent years with Jesus, and so this isn't a quick-fix plan. It means walking alongside people from day to day and helping them in every part of their lives to see things with the eyes of God. If we took Jesus at his word and began to discover how we might do this ourselves, it would transform the Church as we know it.
- 'all nations': the word translated 'nations' is *ethne*, meaning tribes or groups of people. We are to go to people who are different from ourselves and enable them to hear the good news too. This means welcoming those who may be different from us to our churches and going to places in our parishes and neighbourhoods where there isn't a Christian presence.
- 'baptizing them in the name of the Father and of the Son and of the Holy Spirit': disciple-making is not just for people inside the Church but also for those who are far from God, so that they might discover who he is and

become Christians. Then they can be baptized and welcomed into the Church.

- 'teaching them to obey everything that I have commanded you': the call is for us to pass on what we have received. There are expert teachers, but all of us can be involved as teaching assistants.

There are so many people who helped me in my journey of faith and discipleship. My parents brought me up in the faith; my children's church leaders prayed for me; a friend called Jonathan prayed for me at school; my university friends Philippa and Tim invited me to the church where my faith came alive and I decided to follow Jesus for myself; church leaders John, Nicky and Sandy helped me grow in my faith; and my wife, Louie, keeps encouraging me to grow.

- 'And remember, I am with you always, to the end of the age': perhaps this is the best part of Jesus' commission to every disciple. It is that he will never leave us. He is with us every step of the way!

## Action

Reflect on who helped you to grow as a disciple of Jesus. Ask yourself, 'Who am I discipling?' If you are helping someone, ask them, 'Who are you discipling?' That is the multiplier. If you are not discipling someone, ask Jesus, 'Who can I help to follow you?' Pray for them. Encourage them. Tell them what you are learning about Jesus. And ask questions about their own faith journey.

## Prayer

Lord Jesus, thank you for those who have helped me to follow you. Please show me who I can help to follow you. May they grow more and more in their knowledge and depth of understanding of who you are and all you have done for them. May they in turn tell others. For the sake of your kingdom. Amen.

# 16

# Feed my sheep

When they had finished breakfast, Jesus said to Simon Peter, 'Simon son of John, do you love me more than these?' He said to him, 'Yes, Lord; you know that I love you.' Jesus said to him, 'Feed my lambs.' A second time he said to him, 'Simon son of John, do you love me?' He said to him, 'Yes, Lord; you know that I love you.' Jesus said to him, 'Tend my sheep.' He said to him the third time, 'Simon son of John, do you love me?' Peter felt hurt because he said to him the third time, 'Do you love me?' And he said to him, 'Lord, you know everything; you know that I love you.' Jesus said to him, 'Feed my sheep. Very truly, I tell you, when you were younger, you used to fasten your own belt and to go wherever you wished. But when you grow old, you will stretch out your hands, and someone else will fasten a belt around you and take you where you do not wish to go.' (He said this to indicate the kind of death by which he would glorify God.) After this he said to him, 'Follow me.'
(John 21.15–19)

David was an unkempt, poor single man in his eighties. He had lived in the same house all his life, and, since his retirement, he had walked the same route every day to buy his paper, milk and other provisions. Each day, he walked past a church. It was part of the local scenery, a quaint old building, but it had nothing to do with him. He just walked past it every day, head down, no one saying hello to him – same old, same old, same old.

One morning as he walked past the church, Fred, one of the congregation members, was out in the church garden pruning some of the bushes. 'Morning,' he called out as David shuffled past. David stopped dead and looked up. 'Morning' came the cry again from Fred. David shuffled over to see what Fred was doing. You see, David loved gardening, and he went closer to get a better look at what was going on. Fred and David then began a conversation, sharing stories and telling each other something of their lives. David was then invited into the church for a cup of coffee. This was unheard of: no one ever took notice of David or invited him to anything.

Six months and several cups of coffee later, David was baptized and confirmed. It was a church where testimony was shared on a regular basis, and when it came to his turn David shuffled up to the front of the church. He took out a piece of paper on which he had put together his words but then folded it back into his pocket. He stared at the congregation for a while and then said,

Thank you. I walked past this church hundreds of times, knowing that this was not for me. But now I have received love and forgiveness. I am the same but different. I have been changed by love. Now please, love each other, just love.

He then made his way back to the font to be baptized. The silence in the church was palpable. The congregation had been met by Jesus.

Jesus' challenge to Peter is poignant. Peter has just denied Jesus three times and watched his friend die upon the cross. Now, Jesus puts Peter on the spot. Three times Peter is asked, 'Do you love me?' and three times he answers, 'Yes, you know I love you.' By the end Peter is getting a little miffed at being asked the same question, but Jesus is ensuring that Peter realizes the importance of his vocation and new calling, one that will be personally very difficult, and will involve Peter being taken where he does not wish to go. His vocation, his calling, was being deliberately transformed from saving his own skin, as he had done on the day of Jesus' crucifixion, to carrying out the will of Jesus Christ, led by the Holy Spirit of Pentecost. Peter becomes a lifelong learner – one of the key attributes of being a Christian is always wanting to learn more – even though this may be painful. And what does this new direction, this new calling, look like? Well, first Jesus says to him, 'Feed my lambs', not the generic sheep. Lambs are small, vulnerable, fragile, young, in need of protection and of special care. Here is Jesus' imperative to care for the poor, vulnerable, those on the margins of society, the unloved and unwanted, and this is to be at the heart of the mission of the Church, personified by love. Earlier Peter had remonstrated with Jesus when it came to his feet being washed, yet now he is called to wash the feet of the unwanted, the vulnerable and the marginalized.

Peter was given a new vocation, a new calling. David also lived out his new calling, his new vocation. Both needed to be lifelong learners, with a heart to understand more of God's great depths of love for his creatures and his creation.

## Action

This Lent, will we let our hearts be changed by an encounter with Jesus, with love personified? Will we be open to such an encounter having consequences for our behaviour as it did for Peter and for David? Let's be honest – being life-long learners and following such a vocation is not for the faint-hearted.

## Prayer

Dear Lord, help me to see every day as a gift from you, and an opportunity to learn something new about you. Help me also to feed your lambs, like Peter. Help me to discern what you are asking of me today, that I may grow, learn and live out your hope in me to the best of my ability. Amen.

Part 3

# ON BEING THE BODY OF CHRIST

# 17

# Many gifts but one Spirit

Now concerning spiritual gifts, brothers and sisters, I do not want you to be uninformed. You know that when you were pagans, you were enticed and led astray to idols that could not speak. Therefore I want you to understand that no one speaking by the Spirit of God ever says 'Let Jesus be cursed!' and no one can say 'Jesus is Lord' except by the Holy Spirit.

Now there are varieties of gifts, but the same Spirit; and there are varieties of services, but the same Lord; and there are varieties of activities, but it is the same God who activates all of them in everyone. To each is given the manifestation of the Spirit for the common good. To one is given through the Spirit the utterance of wisdom, and to another the utterance of knowledge according to the same Spirit, to another faith by the same Spirit, to another gifts of healing by the one Spirit, to another the working of miracles, to another prophecy, to another the discernment of spirits, to another various kinds of tongues, to another the interpretation of tongues. All these are activated by one and the same Spirit, who allots to each one individually just as the Spirit chooses.

(1 Cor. 12.1–11)

Do you have a toolbox with your favourite tools, a kitchen drawer with much loved utensils, a garden shed where each tool is clean and ready to go, a desk drawer full of useful little knick-knacks or a sewing basket full of haberdashery? Many of us collect useful gadgets and tools that make a task easier. Or, perhaps even better, we have a friend who does that from whom we can borrow them! The whole point of tools and gadgets is to make a job easier. When you find a good tool, it makes the task much easier and more enjoyable, and helps you to work more efficiently.

God has a beautiful set of tools that he has given to the Church. Paul calls them gifts of the Spirit, or manifestations of the Spirit, and he is keen for the Church to understand what they are all about (v. 1). These tools are a gift from God for the Church to use. They are 'spiritual gifts'. Why are they so important for the Church?

First, Paul says that they point towards Jesus (vv. 2–3). It is so easy to miss the main thing in our lives, to get caught up in so much detail that we miss what is important. As Stephen Covey writes, 'The main thing is to keep the main thing the main thing!'[1] Spiritual gifts are not an end in themselves. They point towards the One who created them and who gives them – to God himself. So the way in which they are used should be characterized by a recognition that Jesus is Lord. He is the one we worship and honour and follow. So, when we use these gifts, others will be 'wowed' not by the user of the gift but by the giver of the gift. They will point towards Jesus.

Second, there is a huge variety of spiritual gifts (vv. 4–6). I think Paul talks about this variety because we sometimes get competitive or possessive, and that becomes destructive. We may look at others and think that they are better than us, or the reverse, that what I'm doing is more significant – and important – than what others are doing. Both views lead us away from God and towards a destructive competitiveness with one another. Instead St Paul says to look at where these gifts come from – they are from one and the same Lord. All of them are important and special and significant. It is not about you: it is about him. We are not to compare; rather we are to appreciate and welcome each gift.

Third, they are a gift to benefit everyone. These gifts are given to each one for the common good (v. 7). Everyone is included because the Spirit wants each one of us to be involved in his work. Each gift is given by a generous God who gives them to us freely. We cannot earn them or work hard for them. They are given as a gift to be received. And they are to be used for the common good, not for individual gain. These are beautiful gifts, distributed by God's Spirit, to everyone so that they can be used to benefit everyone.

It is sometimes said that Church can be like a football match: 22,000 desperately in need of exercise watching twenty-two people in need of a rest. Church is not supposed to be a few people doing everything, but everyone involved in building up the whole body of the Church. And that is why God has given these gifts to the Church for the common good – so that everyone benefits.

Paul then goes on to list a wonderful variety of gifts in verses 8–11. It is not an exhaustive list, because he lists others elsewhere, but it is interesting that these ones – wisdom, healing and miracles – are dependent on God's supernatural power and presence. How we need these in the Church today!

## Action

What gift or gifts has God given you? Ask him to show you. How can you use it or them to benefit and build up the Church? How can you use your gift(s) to point others towards Jesus? How can you encourage others to discover their gifts and use them?

## Prayer

Lord Jesus, thank you that you are a generous God and that you have given gifts to the Church for the common good. Please help me to discover the gifts you have given me and how I can use them to build up the Church. And help me to draw out and encourage those gifts in others so that all may play their part in your Church. For the sake of your kingdom and your glory. Amen.

## Note

1 Stephen R. Covey, *The Seven Habits of Highly Effective People* (London: Simon & Schuster, 2020).

# 18

# One new humanity

So then, remember that at one time you Gentiles by birth, called 'the uncircumcision' by those who are called 'the circumcision' – a physical circumcision made in the flesh by human hands – remember that you were at that time without Christ, being aliens from the commonwealth of Israel, and strangers to the covenants of promise, having no hope and without God in the world. But now in Christ Jesus you who once were far off have been brought near by the blood of Christ. For he is our peace; in his flesh he has made both groups into one and has broken down the dividing wall, that is, the hostility between us. He has abolished the law with its commandments and ordinances, so that he might create in himself one new humanity in place of the two, thus making peace, and might reconcile both groups to God in one body through the cross, thus putting to death that hostility through it. (Eph. 2.11–16)

Paul describes the extraordinary integration in Jesus Christ of those who were previously divided: the circumcised and the uncircumcised, Jews and Gentiles. Although in some places these separations and tensions continue, other divisions are now more prominent across the world. Tom Wright, in an introduction to Ephesians, broadens out Paul's celebration of this new unity, showing its relevance for Christians in every place and age. 'If our churches are still divided in any way along racial or cultural lines,' Wright notes, '[Paul] would say that our gospel, our very grasp of the meaning of Jesus' death, is called into question.'[1]

There are many things today that still divide both Church and society. Churches have not begun to come to terms with the institutional racism that was allowed to alienate the Windrush generation and which still stands in the way of people of different cultures and ethnicities, preventing them from fulfilling their God-given potential in ministry. In society, people are disadvantaged in their access to education, health care, housing and employment because of cultural and ethnic differences. Higher numbers of black and ethnic minorities are either homeless or live in crowded, multi-generational housing and are in insecure jobs. The global COVID-19 pandemic has also disproportionately hurt and killed these people from ethnic minority backgrounds.

In this context, what does it mean to say that Christ is our peace and that in his flesh he has broken down hostility between us? What does it mean to be part of a new humanity? We start by recognizing that we are all connected. No one's choices are purely individual, and our actions reverberate around the world. Climate change, which is exacerbated by our affluent lifestyles, excessive consumption and ever-increasing global travel, disproportionately affects the world's poorest. Global pandemics rip through overcrowded housing with poor sanitation, hurting those who cannot self-isolate or afford medical care. Although we may all be in the same ocean, some of us have better boats with which to weather the storm.

Christ's death and resurrection, themselves crisis and *kairos* moments, herald different ways of belonging. Paul sees how these events bring about radical new integration – of Jew and Gentile, and more broadly of those who were far off and those who were near.

Through the deep, dark suffering and the long Lent of the 2020 global pandemic, small signs of resurrection hope emerged: impromptu music concerts taking place on neighbourhood balconies, practical care being offered to the isolated, restaurants providing banquets to the homeless, clapping for carers, valuing teachers, recognizing key workers instead of celebrities, breathing cleaner air, eventually shopping more carefully and wasting less food.

If Christ is still our peace, and if his flesh still breaks down division and hostility, then there is an immediate task for Christians now, in response to this global crisis, to advocate for policies that put peace and health at the heart of decision-making. In London, when it became clear that the COVID-19 pandemic would spread like wildfire among rough sleepers, temporary accommodation was provided for them in the capital's hotels. That kind of short-term response needs now to be turned into long-term provision, along with making land and property available for those who are vulnerably housed and whose health is precarious. When we belong together as one new humanity, there is no excuse for maintaining walls of exclusion: open hearts need to equal open doors.

For the Church to advocate for such change, it will also need to attend to its own transformation. Paul called the early Christian communities to become radical, inclusive missionary movements for people of every culture and ethnicity. They were not to be believers' clubs and they were to put to death hostility between believers of different traditions. Clearly, we still have work to do.

We have all been brought near through Christ. How do we enact this truth in church and advocate for this truth in the world?

## Action

Engage with a Christian charity that has a global perspective, via online or printed material. In prayer, ask God to use your imagination to help you empathize with the people they support. Be attentive to how God uses this engagement to help you consider how you might act now: perhaps through giving time or money, or through advocacy. Be attentive also to how God is asking you to change, enlarging your humanity in a way that affects your relationships at home, at work and in church.

## Prayer

We are no longer strangers or aliens.
Through Christ you draw us close
and we have hope.
Tear down the divisions that we tolerate
in our churches
and across the world.
So that, as we find our home in you,

strangers may become friends
and hope may be shared.
Amen.

## Note

1  Tom Wright, *Paul for Everyone: The prison letters –
   Ephesians, Philippians, Colossians and Philemon*
   (London: SPCK, 2002), p. 27.

# 19

# The bond of peace

I therefore, the prisoner in the Lord, beg you to lead
a life worthy of the calling to which you have been
called, with all humility and gentleness, with patience,
bearing with one another in love, making every effort
to maintain the unity of the Spirit in the bond of peace.
There is one body and one Spirit, just as you were called
to the one hope of your calling, one Lord, one faith, one
baptism, one God and Father of all, who is above all
and through all and in all.
(Eph. 4.1–6)

In the ninth chapter of the Acts of the Apostles, we read an
account of a remarkable conversion to Christ. Saul – as he is
then called – has been vigorously persecuting the disciples
of Jesus. Journeying along the road to Damascus, Saul falls
to the ground as a brilliant light from heaven shines around
him, and he hears a voice saying, 'Saul, Saul, why are you
persecuting me?' Saul asks, 'Who are you, Lord?' The reply
comes, 'I am Jesus, whom you are persecuting' (v. 5).

In persecuting his disciples, Jesus tells Saul, he is persecuting Jesus himself: disciple and master are one, what is
done to one is done to the other also. We can imagine Paul
(the name he takes after his conversion) pondering long and
deeply on this close identification which has been revealed

to him between Jesus and his followers, between Jesus and the Church: so close indeed as to mean that the life of the one is truly the life of the other.

One very helpful way to understand the letter to the Ephesians, which is panoramic in its theological scope and argument, is to read it as the fruit of St Paul's meditation on his conversion experience and on the words Jesus spoke to him. The letter addresses the mystery of Christ and the mystery of the Church, and the unity – a key term in Ephesians – that exists between the two, a unity in which the individual believer participates by means of faith and baptism.

The passage that we are thinking about now, the opening verses of Ephesians chapter 4, consists of just one sentence in the Greek text, but falls neatly into two parts. Verses 1–3 consist of teaching about the basic Christian virtues, the behaviours that should characterize those who have been called into new life in Christ. The first virtue that Paul names is humility, which is also singled out by him as the fundamental characteristic of the believer in the letter to the Philippians (2.3). Gentleness (or meekness) and patience (or longsuffering) are among the fruits of the Spirit that Paul lists in the letter to the Galatians (5.2). Christians are to bear with one another in love and, crucially for the overall picture of the life in Christ and life in the Church painted in the letter, they are not to be quarrelsome, but to do all they can to preserve that unity which is the Spirit's gift 'in the bond of peace'.

This exhortation to maintain unity leads into the theologically dense but rich second part of the passage. Paul sounds three notes which together make up a single chord that resonates with this theme of unity: 'one body and one Spirit'; 'one Lord, one faith, one baptism'; and 'one God and Father of all'. In so doing he draws together the three persons of the Trinity ('one Spirit . . . one Lord . . . one God') with the Church ('one baptism') and the Christian virtues of hope and faith. Unity in faith, worship and conduct are all brought together, and all flow not simply from ethical choices or speculative reasoning but from a living reality: the life of God the Holy Trinity in the Church.

Reflecting on these demanding but profound verses from Ephesians helps us to deal with two mistakes that can creep into our understanding of the Christian life. The first is the suggestion that there is such a thing as a 'churchless Christianity'. For Paul, we can never be Christians alone but only as we are part of the living body, the Church. The second mistake is that disunity in the body of Christ is something that we must simply put up with, or accept as an inevitable and permanent state of affairs. Paul teaches us both that unity is God's gift and that it is an essential (and not merely incidental) part of the vocation of Christians to maintain the full, visible unity of the community of those who have been baptized into Christ and share a common faith in him.

## Action

Pray for the unity of Christ's Church, that it may truly be an instrument of unity and reconciliation for the sake of the world.

## Prayer

Lord Jesus Christ,
who said to your Apostles:
Peace I leave you, my peace I give you,
look not on our sins,
but on the faith of your Church,
and graciously grant her peace and unity
in accordance with your will.
Who live and reign for ever and ever.
Amen.
(Communion Rite, Roman Catholic Liturgy of the Mass)

# 20

# How often do we forgive?

Then Peter came and said to him, 'Lord, if another member of the church sins against me, how often should I forgive? As many as seven times?'
(Matt. 18.21)

The advent of modern media has greatly increased the possibility of seeing some very disturbing images. You may recall the beheading of the journalist James Foley some years ago in retaliation for US air strikes on so-called Islamic State targets in Iraq. More recently we have seen pictures of terrorist events in London, Manchester, Nice and Barcelona.

Media footage following such events often raises the question of forgiveness and, more rarely, calls for retribution. For example, the beheading of James Foley caused Frank Gardner on BBC Radio 4 to argue that such acts could be powerful in influencing vulnerable young men by presenting a compelling narrative of oppression and the need for revenge.[1]

You may also recall the vicar who resigned in 2006, a year after her daughter was killed in a terrorist attack in London. The Revd Julia Nicholson said: 'It's very difficult to stand behind an altar and lead people in words of peace and reconciliation and forgiveness when I feel very far from that myself.'[2]

I don't know what your reaction is to these stories. I have never been bombed out of my home. I have not lost my daughter to a terrorist attack. I have never had to leave my home, taking nothing with me, to protect my family. In practical terms I have little insight into how I would react faced with similar situations. Could I forgive? Could I turn the other cheek? Could I forgive not just once but seven times, let alone seventy-seven times, in such complex situations?

In our Gospel reading Peter asks the question, 'Lord, if another member of the church sins against me, how often should I forgive?' Interestingly he does not ask whether or not he should forgive, but rather how far he needs to go. By offering to forgive seven times, he undoubtedly thinks he is doing a lot. And he is right: forgiving the same mistake seven times is a lot.

Peter and the other disciples must have been surprised at Jesus' reply: 'Not seven times, but seventy-seven times' (Matt. 18.22). In other words, without limit, without counting. Jesus Christ wants us to understand that God's forgiveness is not reasonable but unbelievable, that it flies in the face of common sense and is beyond all calculation. It is impossible to understand the forgiveness we are to show one another without beginning to comprehend God's forgiveness of us.

Jesus Christ holds up a mirror to us each time we think we have to limit our forgiveness. In the parable of the unforgiving servant that follows this command, the comment of the king is our King's word to us: 'Should you not have had mercy on your fellow-slave, as I had mercy on you?' (Matt. 18.33).

The Northern Ireland peace process gives us an insight into how some have put this into practice. The Revd Peter Price, in his book *Undersong*, reflects that reconciliation often began with informal encounters between individuals from different communities.[3] It was only when they had the courage to listen to each other's stories that they began to see areas of commonality and, in that commonality, they began to find an ability to lay aside their prejudice, their jealousies and their anger and ambitions.

Thinking about the big issues that require reconciliation in the world must not cause us to forget our own hearts and communities. Perhaps we should start within ourselves – finding peace with God and then the reconciliation that is required within the Church.

Whatever context we have in view, true reconciliation and forgiveness are perhaps the hardest task for humanity to achieve. Let us therefore look to our relationship with God, rooted in his forgiveness, and seek to forgive – because therein lies the peace of the Church.

## Action

Is there anyone you need to forgive? Could you reach out to them today?

## Prayer

Merciful Lord,
absolve your people from their offences,
so that through your bountiful goodness
we may all be delivered from the chains of those sins
which by our frailty we have committed;

grant this, heavenly Father,
for Jesus Christ's sake, our blessed Lord and Saviour,
who is alive and reigns with you,
in the unity of the Holy Spirit,
one God, now and for ever.
Amen.
(Collect for Lent, *Common Worship*)

## Notes

1 Frank Gardner, interviewed on the *Today* programme, BBC Radio 4, 20 August 2014, <www.bbc.co.uk/news/world-middle-east-28867627>.

2 'Vicar struggles to forgive the terrorists who killed her daughter', *Independent*, 7 March 2006, <www.independent.co.uk/news/uk/this-britain/vicar-struggles-to-forgive-the-terrorists-who-killed-her-daughter-6107339.html>.

3 Peter B. Price, *Undersong* (London: Darton, Longman & Todd, 2002).

# 21

# One as we are one

'I ask not only on behalf of these, but also on behalf of
those who will believe in me through their word, that
they may all be one. As you, Father, are in me and I am
in you, may they also be in us, so that the world may
believe that you have sent me. The glory that you have
given me I have given them, so that they may be one,
as we are one, I in them and you in me, that they may
become completely one, so that the world may know
that you have sent me and have loved them even as you
have loved me.'
(John 17.20–23)

One of the easiest ways to get a group of clergy talking is to
ask them to share funeral stories. Everyone who has taken
funerals will have a story to tell. Often, these involve recount-
ing stories of dysfunctional families who have fallen out
with one another, secrets that had been revealed belatedly or
judgement on how someone has behaved in the past.

Such conversations can turn into a competition as to who
has the best story. Reality may be embellished to prove a
point, and the dysfunctional nature of the reality of some
people's lives may be exaggerated.

But clergy, of course, are not unique in this. A cursory
look at Jeremy Kyle, Judge Rinder, Tricia, Oprah and Jerry

Springer shows that some have built their careers on airing family secrets and dysfunctional relations. This is usually to the delight of a whooping audience, who feel that at least their reality is not quite as bad as those being portrayed on the screen or in front of them.

The church family too is not exempt from being dysfunctional. This can be revealed in all sorts of power plays in the Church, often through battles over worship styles, seating, liturgy, coffee and the place of children's ministry. This inability to agree is not confined to inward disagreement, but is often directed outwards at the diocese, the bishop, the government or whoever it may be. Sometimes it can be played out in a very public digital arena on social media. Pope Francis reminds us in Gaudete et Exsultate that

> Christians too can be caught up in networks of verbal violence through the internet and the various forums of digital communication. Even in Catholic media, limits can be overstepped, defamation and slander can become commonplace, and all ethical standards and respect for the good name of others can be abandoned. The result is a dangerous dichotomy, since things can be said there that would be unacceptable in public discourse, and people look to compensate for their own discontent by lashing out at others.[1]

But let's be honest, all human beings are dysfunctional, and to be in a state of conflict with one another is the most natural thing in the world. We are fragile and mixed-up creatures, a bundle of contradictions that we spend a lifetime negotiating and navigating alongside the contradictions of everyone else. Some therapists describe this as a kind of dance in which we all participate.

In his excellent book *The Divine Dance* Richard Rohr speaks of God's generosity in drawing us into the dance of the Trinity. In the power of the Spirit, we can partake of the dynamic relationship between the Father and the Son, a relationship that is revealed to us in John chapter 17, the private priestly prayer of Jesus. Jesus has spoken in his final discourses that night before he died, and now in chapter 17 he raises his eyes to heaven and prays for unity, that we may be one. This shows something of the uniqueness of Jesus Christ, the one through whom all things came into being, who will, the following day, draw all things to himself when he defeats death itself. This same Jesus will ascend to God, taking our transformed humanity with him and enabling us to live in forgiven unity. John chapter 17 therefore reminds us of God's soul and reveals crucial moments for a Christian. Our response must be to forgive as we ourselves are forgiven, even when there is difficulty and conflict in the air.

In the world, in our communities, in our homes and in our churches, we will find conflict. Sometimes it is terrible conflict. But at Lent we again come face to face with the cross, and are reminded of our need to forgive each other, to confess when our vanity has been more important to us than God's generosity, and to live with the confidence of Jesus' forgiveness and hope for reconciliation each day. This is not easy, and it takes a lifetime of work. It requires the Church to enable truth to be told, and not a truth that has been honed and sanctioned in advance. This truth can be uncomfortable, and it requires immeasurable levels of listening to enable the truth to set the Church free.

## Action

How could I hear truth that might be uncomfortable today? Are there people on the edge of church life whom I could be better at listening to?

## Prayer

Dear Lord, all too often I am engulfed in my own thoughts, desires, hopes and dreams. Yet I recognize that on my own I add to the dysfunctionality of the world. Help me to dance your divine dance, to seek your truth and to live out my life in the power of your forgiveness. Help me also to show forgiveness to others, as we strive for the unity that Jesus prays for and that the cross makes a reality. Amen.

## Note

1 Gaudete et Exsultate, Ch. 4, 115, <www.vatican.va/content/francesco/en/apost_exhortations/documents/papa-francesco_esortazione-ap_20180319_gaudete-et-exsultate.html#PERSEVERANCE,_PATIENCE_AND_MEEKNESS>.

# 22

# Citizenship in heaven

Brothers and sisters, join in imitating me, and observe those who live according to the example you have in us. For many live as enemies of the cross of Christ; I have often told you of them, and now I tell you even with tears. Their end is destruction; their god is the belly; and their glory is in their shame; their minds are set on earthly things. But our citizenship is in heaven, and it is from there that we are expecting a Saviour, the Lord Jesus Christ. He will transform the body of our humiliation so that it may be conformed to the body of his glory, by the power that also enables him to make all things subject to himself. Therefore, my brothers and sisters, whom I love and long for, my joy and crown, stand firm in the Lord in this way, my beloved. (Phil. 3.17—4.1)

A few years ago, we were in the USA, visiting San Francisco. We spent a few hours wandering around Chinatown in the north-east corner of the city. It was, to be honest, a disorientating experience. A few moments before, we had been in a very American city, with office blocks, bars, hot-dog stands and the rest. Suddenly, now it felt as if we were in Asia, with the smells of spicy food, Chinese spoken all around us and all the writing in an alien script. Like Chinatown in cities all over the world, there are enclaves of other cultures, people who live in one culture, yet trying at the same time to keep alive the memory of their home.

This is the picture St Paul paints here of the Church's place in the world. It lives in a kind of foreign land, a society whose ways and customs are unfamiliar and strange. Yet its true home is elsewhere – a 'citizenship in heaven'. Heaven in the Bible is the place where God dwells. It is not so much a place in the sky somewhere as a different dimension, if we can imagine that – around us and present at all times, though not visible to our ordinary senses and only accessed by faith, prayer, the Holy Scriptures and the sacraments as 'portals' into the dwelling place of God. Like those Chinese residents of San Francisco, or exiles in any great city, the Church lives with its feet planted in the territory of this world, a world that is often experienced as enemy territory, yet with its true home and true loyalty elsewhere.

Like exiles, or resident aliens, the Church is invested in the society in which it lives, and works for its good whether in London, Leicester or Lima. The Old Testament exiles in Babylon were told to 'seek the welfare of the city where I have sent you into exile, and pray to the Lord on its behalf, for in its welfare you will find your welfare' (Jer. 29.7). So the Church does the same. Yet, while doing that, it tries to remind the city of its true homeland. Exiles cook the food, speak the language of their home, even when they are far from home. They live in this sometimes uncomfortable overlap between the place where they live and their true home.

The kingdom of heaven is a place that operates by a different set of customs and rules from those of the societies we live in. It is a place that operates by different rules, that sings a different song and breathes a different air. In this kingdom, the rich are no more valued than the poor, those who mourn are counted blessed and it is the merciful rather than the opinionated who are prized most highly. The Church seeks the welfare of its neighbours but not just by trying to help them a little, but by trying to give them a taste of their homeland, which is in fact the place where the whole human race was intended to find a home.

## Action

Try to imagine yourself as an exile, living and being committed to the neighbourhood where you live and work, yet with your true home in heaven. Do what you can to give others a taste of heaven – by an act of inexplicable kindness, a gift of sudden generosity, an offer to pray for someone or by daring to speak up for those who have no voice.

## Prayer

Our Father in heaven, our true home is with you. Yet we live here in this world that you have made and that so often does not reflect your love. Help us today to live as citizens of heaven, spreading around us the language and aromas of our heavenly home. Amen.

# 23

# On honouring the poor

My brothers and sisters, do you with your acts of favouritism really believe in our glorious Lord Jesus Christ? For if a person with gold rings and in fine clothes comes into your assembly, and if a poor person in dirty clothes also comes in, and if you take notice of the one wearing the fine clothes and say, 'Have a seat here, please', while to the one who is poor you say, 'Stand there', or, 'Sit at my feet', have you not made distinctions among yourselves, and become judges with evil thoughts? Listen, my beloved brothers and sisters. Has not God chosen the poor in the world to be rich in faith and to be heirs of the kingdom that he has promised to those who love him? But you have dishonoured the poor. Is it not the rich who oppress you? Is it not they who drag you into court? Is it not they who blaspheme the excellent name that was invoked over you?
(James 2.1–7)

In the years after Jesus' death and resurrection and the coming of the Spirit, the early Church had to work out how they should live. What were to be the distinctive marks of what it meant to be a follower of Jesus Christ, both for individuals and for the Christian community? So, probably about ten or fifteen years after Pentecost, here is James the Just, the Lord's brother, writing to Christians who have converted from Judaism, putting down some markers and answering some questions which were clearly already being asked in these early Christian communities.

The pattern of James's approach is to insist that faith must work itself out in our actions ('faith by itself, if it has no works, is dead', James 2.17) and that living in that way will bring us to Christian maturity. There's nothing incompatible between James's understanding and that of the rest of the New Testament: he starts with the absolute insistence that it is by faith that we come into relationship with God. But he is unafraid to ask the question 'If you were on trial for being a Christian, would there be enough evidence to convict you?' That's the theme that he explores throughout his letter.

James isn't therefore asking hypothetical questions in today's reading. Here is a real-life situation – Christians showing favouritism and privileging rich people over poor people in their welcome. Surely it is not something we would do in this day and age. I'm not so sure about that. Talk to Caribbean Anglicans of the Windrush generation about the sort of welcome they received in our churches when they first came to the UK. Consider the churches (not ours, of course) that claim to be welcoming fellowships but studiously ignore strangers when they roll up at the door. Think about how our churches treat folk who are 'not like us' today.

James deals with the issue head-on. First, it's inconsistent. It doesn't fit with our faith in Jesus Christ, 'our glorious Lord' (v. 1), who teaches that God loves all without distinction (v. 4; see Romans 3.22–23; 10.12). Second, it's illogical (see vv. 5–7), for it was the rich (to whom they were showing favouritism) who were dragging members of their congregation through the courts. Why would you discriminate in favour of your persecutors? He also goes on to argue in verses 8 and 9 that it's against the law of God, because it breaks the command to love our neighbour as ourselves, thereby wreaking havoc on all the commandments.

Note, incidentally, how much James's words here run in parallel with Matthew's version of the Sermon on the Mount in chapter 7. Some have suggested that James was working from source material that drew on the sermon when he wrote this letter.

Discrimination based on class and wealth is contrary to Christian profession, for the poor, James argues, are our teachers (v. 5). One of the challenges for the Christian Church is the way we seem to have failed to learn this lesson over many centuries. The Bishop of Burnley, Philip North, once described the Church of England as being 'complicit in the abandonment of the poor'.[1] There is a structural as well as a congregational way of favouring the rich over the poor. There are unavoidable questions about the resources that churches allocate to work on our most deprived estates, and about our priorities in mission.

## Action

What changes do we need to make in the ways in which our churches and congregations operate to ensure that we treat the poor, the outsider and the stranger with proper respect? How much does that spill over into our attitudes and actions in the wider political sphere? What might we ask the

Holy Spirit to do in our lives so that we reflect the law of Christ in our relations with our neighbours? What are the big questions about how the Church deploys its resources?

## Prayer

Almighty God,
teach us to serve the perfect law of freedom.
Give us grace to live without partiality,
to serve without hesitancy
and to love unconditionally
as servants of the excellent name of him to whom we
    belong,
Jesus Christ our Lord. Amen.

## Note

1 Quoted by Madeleine Davies, 'Church is "abandoning" the poorest areas, Bishop Philip North warns', *Church Times*, 11 August 2017, <www.churchtimes.co.uk/articles/2017/11-august/news/uk/church-is-abandoning-the-poorest-areas-bishop-warns>.

# 24

# One body in Christ

I appeal to you therefore, brothers and sisters, by the mercies of God, to present your bodies as a living sacrifice, holy and acceptable to God, which is your spiritual worship. Do not be conformed to this world, but be transformed by the renewing of your minds, so that you may discern what is the will of God – what is good and acceptable and perfect.

For by the grace given to me I say to everyone among you not to think of yourself more highly than you ought to think, but to think with sober judgement, each according to the measure of faith that God has assigned. For as in one body we have many members, and not all the members have the same function, so we, who are many, are one body in Christ, and individually we are members one of another. We have gifts that differ according to the grace given to us: prophecy, in proportion to faith; ministry, in ministering; the teacher, in teaching; the exhorter, in exhortation; the giver, in generosity; the leader, in diligence; the compassionate, in cheerfulness.

(Rom. 12: 1–8)

In his letter to the Romans, St Paul sets out his great narrative arc of how fallen humanity is saved in Christ (chapters

1–8), and then addresses the specific question of how the people of Israel, God's first covenant people, are themselves included in God's redeeming work in Christ (chapters 9–11). Now, in the third and final section of this the longest of his epistles, St Paul turns to the question of Christian living.

He begins (12.1) by reaching for the language of cult, inviting the Christians in Rome to offer 'spiritual worship' (Greek *latreia*, a word that has a definite connotation of liturgical worship), by means of the 'living sacrifice' of themselves, holy and acceptable to God. Through his use of the terminology of priesthood, worship and sacrifice, Paul teaches his readers to understand themselves to be a priestly people. Christian life and worship go together, and both have a sacrificial character because both depend on the sacrifice of Christ himself.

In his first letter to the Corinthians, St Paul writes, within a very short space about the Eucharist and about the character of the Christian community, using the metaphor of the body (1 Cor. 11—12). Here in Romans (composed after 1 Corinthians), Paul returns to the image of the body, and sets it in the context of a longer passage which reflects on the qualities and characteristics that should be the hallmarks of Christian living. While in the Romans text Paul does not write explicitly about the Eucharist, the parallels with his train of thought in 1 Corinthians and his use of the language of liturgical worship already noted can lead us reasonably to conclude that the Eucharist was not far from his mind when he composed Romans 12.

This holding together of Christian worship with Christian living is very important. It is a corrective to two possible errors that can creep into our understanding of what it means to be a Christian. The first mistake is to suggest that being a Christian can be defined by leading a 'good life', serving others, making the right choices and observing the moral law. The problem here is the omission of the dimension of worship, of the calling to participate in the liturgy of the New Covenant (the Eucharist), that perfect offering of spiritual sacrifices to God. The reverse mistake is to fail to realize that right worship must flow into right living: the offering of worship (and particularly the celebration of the Eucharist) can never be isolated from every aspect of the life of the body, and every member of the body has his or her part to play.

A good test of any Christian community may be to assess its life and character in the light of what Paul writes in Romans 12. Is the liturgy at the centre of its life, celebrated with care, beauty and dignity? Is there a diversity of members of the body in this particular local manifestation of the Church, each bringing his or her own gifts and calling for the better flourishing of the whole? Does the life of this eucharistic community bear fruit in Christ-likeness, in personal growth in holiness, in sacrificial living? Does it play a part in the life of the wider Church responsibly and generously, and does it extend a welcome to all in Christ's name? (Rom. 12.13).

## Action

Spend some time, perhaps by yourself or in company with fellow worshippers, considering your own local church or worshipping community in the light of these thoughts.

## Prayer

A prayer of Bishop Thomas Ken (1637–1711) after Holy Communion:

> Glory be to thee, O Jesus, my Lord and my God, for thus feeding my soul with thy most blessed body and blood. Oh, let thy heavenly food transfuse new life and new vigour into my soul, and into the souls of all that communicate with me, that our faith may daily increase; that we may all grow more humble and contrite for our sins; that we may all love thee and serve thee, and praise thee more fervently, more incessantly, than ever we have done heretofore. Amen.[1]

## Note

1 *The Complete Book of Christian Prayer* (London: Continuum, 1996), p. 351.

Part 4

# BECOMING MORE CHRIST-LIKE

# 25

# Let the word of Christ dwell in you richly

So if you have been raised with Christ, seek the things that are above, where Christ is, seated at the right hand of God. Set your minds on things that are above, not on things that are on earth, for you have died, and your life is hidden with Christ in God. When Christ who is your life is revealed, then you also will be revealed with him in glory.

Put to death, therefore, whatever in you is earthly: fornication, impurity, passion, evil desire, and greed (which is idolatry). On account of these the wrath of God is coming on those who are disobedient. These are the ways you also once followed, when you were living that life. But now you must get rid of all such things – anger, wrath, malice, slander, and abusive language from your mouth. Do not lie to one another, seeing that you have stripped off the old self with its practices and have clothed yourselves with the new self, which is being renewed in knowledge according to the image of its creator. In that renewal there is no longer Greek and Jew, circumcised and uncircumcised, barbarian, Scythian, slave and free; but Christ is all and in all!

As God's chosen ones, holy and beloved, clothe yourselves with compassion, kindness, humility, meekness,
and patience. Bear with one another and, if anyone has
a complaint against another, forgive each other; just as
the Lord has forgiven you, so you also must forgive.
Above all, clothe yourselves with love, which binds
everything together in perfect harmony. And let the
peace of Christ rule in your hearts, to which indeed
you were called in the one body. And be thankful. Let
the word of Christ dwell in you richly; teach and admonish one another in all wisdom; and with gratitude
in your hearts sing psalms, hymns, and spiritual songs
to God.
(Col. 3.1–16)

We are all capable of entertaining desires and of acting in
ways that are deeply harmful to others and to ourselves.
In Colossians Paul is clear that fornication, impurity, passion, evil desire and greed need to be put to death. Those
who disobey will be subject to God's wrath.

It is right that everyone hears these hard words and that
we do not soften them in any way. It is also right that insti-
tutions hear them, particularly churches that have not been
honest in facing up to the abuse perpetrated by their own
ministers. Clergy abuse always involves an imbalance of
power and an abuse of trust. These exacerbate the damage
that is already caused when inappropriate sexual relationships are formed within the context of ministry. Churches
have been poor at investigating, acknowledging and making reparation for these breaches of boundaries and of trust.

Transparency and accountability have not been properly valued, and survivors of clergy abuse have been left to recover from their wounds with neither acknowledgement nor support.

The Christian life involves forming our lives around the pattern of Christ. There is no place within that reformation for abusive, deceitful or dishonest behaviour: our old selves need to be stripped of anything that remains of such practices and to put on new clothing. This new clothing, which is to be renewed in knowledge, surely includes integrity, stability and accountability. These need to be worked at, and they bring freedom in Christ.

For those involved in authorized ministry, the bar is set higher. When we take up ministerial roles we are put into situations where there are ample opportunities for transgressing sexual, emotional, financial and spiritual boundaries, as well as boundaries of power, of trust and of confidentiality. In addition, there are privileges and projections that accompany status which are often deeply bound up with people's understanding of and desire for connection with the divine. Our hidden need to be needed, and our genuine desire to be warm and open, generous in giving and receiving, and present with people in their journeys of faith, must remain within carefully managed boundaries. Church settings can contain a heady mix of intense and sensual worship, personal revelation and charismatically powerful leadership which can seem to offer a fleeting impression that God is present in the breaking of boundaries. This is an illusion. The true love that we know in God does not thrive in murky shadows, but is open, faithful and strong. It can stand scrutiny, it will bear the test of time and it does not prey on the weak.

Paul goes on to speak about forgiving those who hurt us. He is largely silent here on how we should seek forgiveness of those we have wounded, whether individually or as part of an institution that has not listened, has not acted and has not changed its ways. However, we are instructed to teach and admonish one another in all wisdom. At an institutional level, this must mean apologizing to those who have been hurt. It must mean building on and better resourcing recent improvements in safeguarding practice. It must also mean responding generously and humbly to survivors of abuse, managing insurance claims with integrity and without dragging our feet.

Personally and institutionally, clothing ourselves with compassion, kindness, humility, meekness and patience is about repenting fully, asking God to renew our hearts and minds, and praying that both our powerful lusts and our lust for power may be transformed into the passionate worship of God in Christ.

## Action

Ask yourself how you are held to account. Consider whether there is a friend, a small group of colleagues, a mentor, a confessor or a spiritual director with whom you are committed to being honest about what tempts you and what you have done wrong. If you need professional help, seek it out now. In that safe space, name what troubles you and seek accountability, forgiveness and amendment of your life.

## Prayer

Loving God, you know my deepest desires;
show me where I need to be healed,
open my eyes to see where your image is being
      wounded,
and give me passion to defend the weak.
Renew each of us in knowledge,
and form your Church in the image of Christ.
Amen.

# 26

# Having the mind of Christ

These things God has revealed to us through the Spirit; for the Spirit searches everything, even the depths of God. For what human being knows what is truly human except the human spirit that is within? So also no one comprehends what is truly God's except the Spirit of God. Now we have received not the spirit of the world, but the Spirit that is from God, so that we may understand the gifts bestowed on us by God. And we speak of these things in words not taught by human wisdom but taught by the Spirit, interpreting spiritual things to those who are spiritual.

Those who are unspiritual do not receive the gifts of God's Spirit, for they are foolishness to them, and they are unable to understand them because they are spiritually discerned. Those who are spiritual discern all things, and they are themselves subject to no one else's scrutiny.

'For who has known the mind of the Lord
    so as to instruct him?'
But we have the mind of Christ.
(1 Cor. 2.10–16)

I wonder if you would say that you are wise? I often reflect that, as a Christian, it is wisdom that I need – wisdom to know how to live my life in the pattern of Christ.

The book of Proverbs tells us that wisdom is more precious than rubies (8.11), fine gold or silver (16.16). It will give us a garland to grace our heads and present us with a glorious crown and an adornment around the neck (4.9). King Solomon was right, when he was offered anything in the whole world, to ask for wisdom. God was so delighted with his answer that he gave him wisdom and everything else as well.

But wisdom isn't just amassing intellectual information or enjoying the elegance of abstract theories. It is Christ crucified that is the wisdom of God (1 Cor. 1.23–24). Wisdom is knowing that, by denying ourselves and taking up our cross and following Jesus Christ, we will find life in all its fullness. Wisdom is knowing that to save our lives we need to lose them.

The wisdom of the cross seems folly to the wisdom of the world (1 Cor. 1.21). Strength in weakness, gaining by losing and the power of the cross still seem foolish to those who measure strength by gross national product and megaton bombs. Those devoted to finishing first, who thrive on power as prominence and who seek knowledge as a source of power will never understand this. Wisdom can't be gained through human endeavour alone.

The wisdom of the cross tells us that when we are willing to give up our identity, to sacrifice our personal freedom, to let go of our prejudices, to stop holding on to material wealth and our allegiance to others, and to die to self, we will inherit the crown of rejoicing, an everlasting name, the kingdom of God and life in all its fullness.

The wisdom that comes from heaven is first of all pure, then peace-loving, considerate, submissive, full of mercy and good fruit, impartial and sincere.

When we put our faith in Christ, he becomes for us 'wisdom from God, and righteousness and sanctification and redemption' (1 Cor. 1.30). Incredibly, this means that we can say that we have the mind of Christ. If that is true there is no depth of cross-shaped wisdom too deep, no height of spiritual knowledge too high, for us to explore.

Isaac Watts reflects this in a verse of his hymn 'Praise ye the Lord':

He formed the stars, those heavenly flames,
He counts their numbers, calls their names;
His wisdom's vast, and knows no bound,
A deep where all our thoughts are drowned.[1]

We therefore need to spend time with him – to abide with him. How often do we rush on and not abide? Is it any surprise then that we struggle to comprehend God and his wisdom?

It has also been suggested that wisdom comes about only when we find time not only to gain knowledge but also for idleness – idleness in the true tradition of the contemplative, which means finding time for reflection, for freedom of thought. The creative wonder of Newton's moment under the apple tree.

We need to find time for reflection, for freedom of thought and creative wonder, to find that place where all our thoughts are drowned.

## Action

Actively try to use time in your day for reflection, whether it is waiting for the kettle to boil, making lunch or going for a walk – find time for 'idleness' in the true tradition of the contemplative.

## Prayer

Lord Jesus, stay with us,
for evening is at hand and the day is past;
be our companion in the way,
kindle our hearts and awaken hope,
that we may know you as you are revealed in
    Scripture
and the breaking of bread.
Grant this for the sake of your love.
Amen.
(Collect for Evening Prayer, *Common Worship*)

## Note

1  <www.hymnwiki.org/Praise_Ye_the_Lord>.

# 27

# Transformed into his image

And all of us, with unveiled faces, seeing the glory of the Lord as though reflected in a mirror, are being transformed into the same image from one degree of glory to another; for this comes from the Lord, the Spirit.

Therefore, since it is by God's mercy that we are engaged in this ministry, we do not lose heart. We have renounced the shameful things that one hides; we refuse to practise cunning or to falsify God's word; but by the open statement of the truth we commend ourselves to the conscience of everyone in the sight of God. And even if our gospel is veiled, it is veiled to those who are perishing. In their case the god of this world has blinded the minds of the unbelievers, to keep them from seeing the light of the gospel of the glory of Christ, who is the image of God. For we do not proclaim ourselves; we proclaim Jesus Christ as Lord and ourselves as your slaves for Jesus' sake. For it is the God who said, 'Let light shine out of darkness', who has shone in our hearts to give the light of the knowledge of the glory of God in the face of Jesus Christ.

But we have this treasure in clay jars, so that it may be made clear that this extraordinary power belongs to God and does not come from us.

(2 Cor. 3.18—4.7)

Ancient mirrors were not as clear as ours. They were always a little hazy and blurred, and yet they could still reflect the image of whatever was in front of them. In this passage, St Paul uses the image of a mirror to describe how we find ourselves growing into the likeness of Christ throughout our lives.

In chapter 3 he has explored the idea that, unlike Moses in the Old Testament, who had to wear a veil over his face so as to avoid being blinded by the light of God, now that God has revealed himself to us in the face of Jesus Christ, we can look 'with unveiled faces, seeing the glory of the Lord' (2 Cor. 3.18). As we look on the glory of Christ, his compassion, his humility, his acts of healing, his teaching, his death and resurrection, we see right before us the image of God (2 Cor. 4.4). As we look at the glory of God revealed in the face of Christ, we will be gradually transformed into his image, just as a mirror takes on the image of what is placed before it.

The fourth-century Christian theologian Gregory of Nyssa used this idea often:

Human nature is very much like a mirror in its ability to change in accordance with the different impressions of its free will. When you put gold in front of a mirror the mirror takes on the appearance of the gold and because of the reflection it shines with the same gleam as the real substance. So too, if it catches the reflection of something loathsome it imitates this ugliness by means of a likeness, as for example of a frog, a toad, a millipede or anything else that is disgusting to look at, thus reproducing in its own substance whatever is placed in front of it.[1]

Whether or not you find toads or millipedes 'loathsome', Gregory's point is that, just as a mirror takes on the colours and shape of whatever is placed before it, so we will tend to take on the shape and image of whatever we put in front of our gaze. Ancient mirrors were made of polished metal and so often showed an image that was a little blurred. This helps our understanding here: we may reflect the image of what we look at imperfectly, but what we look at still determines what happens to our souls.

So it matters what we spend our time looking at. Everything we read or watch on TV, websites, YouTube or Netflix shapes us in small and subtle ways, in a positive or a negative direction. Depending on whom we follow or what fills our feeds, hours spent scrolling through Twitter, Facebook or Instagram can either lift our spirits or twist them into knots.

So the advice of St Paul, and for that matter Gregory and many of the wise Christians of the past, is to make sure we fill our hearts and minds with what is life-giving, truthful, honest and wise. Jesus once said: 'Your eye is the lamp of your body. If your eye is healthy, your whole body is full of light; but if it is not healthy, your body is full of darkness' (Luke 11.34). What you let into your eyes affects your heart more than what goes into your stomach.

In particular this reminds us of the importance of worship. As we come to pay close attention to the God of Jesus Christ day by day and especially when we come together on Sundays, asking the Holy Spirit to make Jesus real to us, we find ourselves slowly being transformed into the image of Christ, who fills our attention. It is a call to us to make a priority of worship, prayer and the reading of the Bible. Yes, there may be times we have to miss our regular acts of worship, but let's try not to get out of the habit of looking intently and regularly into the face of Jesus Christ so that we, like those ancient mirrors, can take on his likeness as we grow into maturity.

## Action

How could your present patterns of worship, prayer and Bible-reading be hindering your Christian growth? What small step could you take to make worship more central in your life?

## Prayer

Lord Jesus Christ, in your face we see the image and glory of God. Help us to keep looking and learning more of you each day so that we become like you in your goodness and love. Amen.

## Note

1 *From Glory to Glory: Texts from Gregory of Nyssa's mystical writings*, ed. Jean Daniélou (Crestwood, NY: St Vladimir's Seminary Press, 2001), p. 171.

# 28

# We shall be like him

See what love the Father has given us, that we should be called children of God; and that is what we are. The reason the world does not know us is that it did not know him. Beloved, we are God's children now; what we will be has not yet been revealed. What we do know is this: when he is revealed, we will be like him, for we will see him as he is. And all who have this hope in him purify themselves, just as he is pure.

(1 John 3.1–3)

'What are you like?' is usually a semi-rhetorical question, uttered in a friendly but derisory tone when the speaker wants to highlight some quirk of their mate's character. For the Christian, it's a question with a bit more gravity to it. John has been warning his readers against those who were seeking to deceive the Church and were denying the incarnation of Christ. In chapter 3 of the letter, he goes into an aside about the true nature and destiny of Christians – what we are *truly* like!

The letters of John are pretty strong stuff. They are polemical, claim apostolic authority and are assured and confident in the faith. They encourage the original readers (and us) to be clear about Jesus Christ and who he is – and about the nature of eternal life. In the midst of this, there is a glorious essay on love (1 John chapter 4). Love is a thread that runs through the letter – and it is the love of God that John uses as his point of departure in chapter 3.

God's love, John says, is what has made it possible for us to become his children. This is not something that is ours by nature – we all bear the image of God – but it is by the grace of God in Jesus Christ: 'That is what we are' (v. 1). The Jesus who taught his disciples to pray 'Our Father' is indeed the incarnate One, and his death and resurrection have made it possible for us to have a new relationship with God whereby we are adopted as his daughters and sons. This is the intimate relationship into which we have been drawn.

It isn't, of course, just about our present relationship with God: it also marks our eternal destiny. We are those who live as Christians in the here and now, but we are also inheritors of eternal life: 'we will be like him, for we will see him as he is' (v. 2).

Christians experience a revelation of God in their lives, for God is a God who speaks and has spoken supremely in Jesus Christ. So, we know God through Christ (though the world does not know him, v. 1). We know him only imperfectly as yet, and our own future selves are not yet apparent either (v. 2), but all will be revealed at the coming of Christ and his inauguration of the new heavens and new earth. That has an ethical dimension too, for our destiny causes us to live differently – to purify ourselves and live lives of holiness, 'just as he is pure' (v. 3).

Our society is one where identity has come to the fore in public life. The emergence of identity politics, defined as a tendency for people of a particular religion, ethnicity or social identity to form exclusive political alliances, has made a huge impact on our public discourse. Christians aren't exempt from that, but it is vital that we capture the key theological understanding that our primary identity is found in Jesus Christ. It's no surprise that 1 John asserts that primary identity as the way to have confidence in the faith in which we have believed: 'little children, abide in him, so that . . . we may have confidence' (1 John 2.28).

What are we like? We are people of hope, marked with the image of Christ and called to be distinctive in our earthly pilgrimage. To live for God is to live differently, to live counter-culturally.

## Action

Reflect on what it means for you to be a daughter or son of God. Whatever your experience of human family (which can, of course, be good or bad), what is the significance for you of being able to call God father? Are there situations you face today where your knowledge that you are a child of God will enable you to deal better with what is coming up?

## Prayer

Almighty God,
in Jesus Christ you have made us your children.
Grant us to live lives worthy of our calling,
and remind us always of our hope and destiny,
that we may purify ourselves as he is pure
and come to see him as he is. Amen.

# 29

# Remain in me

'I am the true vine, and my Father is the vine-grower. He removes every branch in me that bears no fruit. Every branch that bears fruit he prunes to make it bear more fruit. You have already been cleansed by the word that I have spoken to you. Abide in me as I abide in you. Just as the branch cannot bear fruit by itself unless it abides in the vine, neither can you unless you abide in me. I am the vine, you are the branches. Those who abide in me and I in them bear much fruit, because apart from me you can do nothing. Whoever does not abide in me is thrown away like a branch and withers; such branches are gathered, thrown into the fire, and burned. If you abide in me, and my words abide in you, ask for whatever you wish, and it will be done for you.'
(John 15.1–7)

A vicar sat in the church, as he did every week, for his surgery. He sat for an hour each week, and people would come to him to discuss school applications, wedding and baptism arrangements, specific pastoral difficulties, house blessings, prayer matters and so on. The surgeries used to bring in up to about ten people each time, and each request or conversation was very different.

On one occasion, a large man sat quietly waiting for his turn. When he entered the small chapel for his conversation, the vicar noticed that the man's English was poor but that he could speak French fluently. The man was clearly distressed and needed help. He then proceeded to take off his jumper, his shirt, his vest, and then stood there semi-naked. The vicar stood still, feeling frightened and trapped. There was no alarm or panic button. The man then pointed out the scars on his shoulder, back and chest – these scars were bullet holes, and he indicated that he had suffered persecution and had escaped from the Democratic Republic of Congo. He had recently arrived in the parish, and came to the most natural place in the world for help, the Church.

Challenged by this event, the vicar and the wider church community embraced a new partnership with a church in Africa. Several parish trips took place. On every occasion, those who immersed themselves in a different culture, and learned about Jesus Christ in the process, became different and more fervent Christians. In the experience of another's worship, one's encounter with Jesus Christ was transformed back at home. They began to embrace a narrative from other parts of the world, enabling the words and perceptions of others to be shared. It was so refreshing to hear of difference rather than the same people moaning about the same things.

The church was reminded of its unusual material privilege. The average Anglican worldwide is an African woman in her thirties living in sub-Saharan Africa and earning less than $4 a day. The church in London was the exception and not the rule. This realization enabled the church to take the difficult decision to focus its work on young people and to change the way in which it 'looked'.

There were discussions about the way in which decisions were made, who held power and where there was unconscious bias, especially where racism was concerned. This meant, of course, that the church had to (painfully) say goodbye to some of its treasured practices and groups. Far from being mainstream, these were now recognized as displacement activities, and there was a greater intentionality as to who was in leadership and how this was lived out.

Challenged by fellow African Christians, the church significantly developed its discipleship teaching, focusing on telling the stories of Christians around the world. This discipleship led to an increase in confidence, and the church grew enormously. Suddenly the church became a place where so many more people could belong. The biblical theme of the church community stemmed from John chapter 15. Jesus is the vine, we are the branches and the Father is the vine-dresser. All Christians are intimately related through Jesus Christ, as brothers and sisters across the world. We are disciples who are lifelong learners, branches that are related to one another in the one vine. We need one another to be strong, pruned where necessary to prevent displacement activity or a clique mentality, so that we may all have a heart to serve the needs of sisters and brothers both in the locality and also across the world.

## Action

Let's be honest: most of us would feel challenged by the sight of a semi-naked man with bullet holes in his body!

This Lent, what might be our wake-up call? How can we acknowledge our need for one another as Christians across the world? How can we learn from the mission, worship and growth of the Church elsewhere?

## Prayer

Dear Lord, we thank you that you so love the world that you gave us Jesus. We thank you that different peoples and different cultures have so much to learn from one another. By telling our stories, and immersing ourselves in different cultures, we can discover something of the truth. Lord, help us to be open to difference, help us to learn more about you from the unknown, give us hearts of curiosity, and speak profoundly into our imaginations. Amen.

# 30

# Led by the Spirit of God

So then, brothers and sisters, we are debtors, not to the flesh, to live according to the flesh – for if you live according to the flesh, you will die; but if by the Spirit you put to death the deeds of the body, you will live. For all who are led by the Spirit of God are children of God. For you did not receive a spirit of slavery to fall back into fear, but you have received a spirit of adoption. When we cry, 'Abba! Father!' it is that very Spirit bearing witness with our spirit that we are children of God, and if children, then heirs, heirs of God and joint heirs with Christ – if, in fact, we suffer with him so that we may also be glorified with him.
(Rom. 8.12–17)

When Jesus prayed to God he would often use the Aramaic term *Abba*, a term of familiarity and intimacy. Through the pages of the Bible, Jesus is the only one to use this term of God, to indicate the close relationship he experienced with his Father, a relationship that John's Gospel repeatedly describes as the 'only son of the Father'. Jesus alone is entitled to use this particularly intimate word, just as a child is the only one entitled to call their parents 'Mummy' and 'Daddy'.

Yet, it seems that in the earliest churches, Christians were already calling God *Abba* in their prayer and worship. Surely this was presumptuous – surely only Jesus can use that word for God? So how can Christians do this? Paul's answer is that this is in fact a quite natural thing for Christians to do, because the work of the Holy Spirit, which Jesus promised his followers, is to draw us into the same intimacy with the Father as Jesus had. At the heart of God is the deep, unbreakable love between the Father and the Son. The Holy Spirit reaches out to us to beckon us into that love, making us one with Christ (Phil. 2.1) so that we can experience the same deep, intimate love that the Father has for Jesus, his only Son.[1]

There is a difference, however. Jesus is, as it were, the natural son. We are adopted daughters and sons through this Spirit of 'adoption'. My wife's aunt and uncle had five children, three of whom were 'natural', two adopted. Yet when you spent time with the family you realized that there was no difference in how they were treated. The parents showed the same love and devotion to the adopted children as to the natural ones. This is the remarkable picture that St Paul draws here – that, as a follower of Jesus, baptized into union with Christ and filled with the Holy Spirit, we can know ourselves to be as deeply loved by the Father as Jesus was and is.

And yet there is a darker side to this. On the one hand, the Holy Spirit draws us into the same intimate relationship with the Father that Jesus enjoyed, and, on the other hand, he also draws us into the same relationship with the world as Jesus had. Jesus knew the closest possible intimacy with the Father, yet when he entered the world his experience was marked not by welcome but by resistance. In our passage we are told that we are 'joint heirs with Christ – if, in fact, we suffer with him so that we may also be glorified with him' (v. 17).

When we are touched by the Holy Spirit, we should expect the most wonderful, intimate closeness to God, in worship, in our interactions with his creation and in other ways. But we should also expect the same Spirit who led Jesus into the wilderness to do the same with us sometimes. Loving people as Jesus did often hurts.

## Action

As you go about your day, you could consciously think of yourself as an adopted spiritual child, imaging what that means. If you are adopted, you might share with others what that feels like. If you are not, you could ask a friend who has been adopted what it means to them. Similarly, as you think about the struggles you face today, whatever they may be, reflect on the way in which they may be part of the Spirit's work to enable you to suffer with Christ so that you may be glorified with him.

## Prayer

God my Father, I thank you that the Holy Spirit, working in me, enables me to call you Abba, Father, just as Jesus did. Help me to trust your love for me today. And help me to reach out to others with the same love that Jesus showed, even if at times that gets rejected, so that I might grow in likeness to Jesus through the power of the Holy Spirit. Amen.

## Note

1 For more on this, see Graham Tomlin, *The Prodigal Spirit: The Trinity, the Church and the future of the world* (London: Alpha International, 2011).

# 31

# Built into a spiritual house

Rid yourselves, therefore, of all malice, and all guile, insincerity, envy, and all slander. Like newborn infants, long for the pure, spiritual milk, so that by it you may grow into salvation – if indeed you have tasted that the Lord is good.

Come to him, a living stone, though rejected by mortals yet chosen and precious in God's sight, and like living stones, let yourselves be built into a spiritual house, to be a holy priesthood, to offer spiritual sacrifices acceptable to God through Jesus Christ.
(1 Pet. 2.1–5)

When they hear the word 'church', most people will think about an institution or a church building, something that has stood through time, unchanging, unmoving, static and perhaps even a bit old-fashioned. But that is not the picture of the Church in the New Testament. St Peter, whose name means 'the Rock' and was given to him by Jesus, says it is quite the opposite!

As disciples of Jesus we are never to be bystanders. We are called to play an active part in God's purposes. Peter describes the Church as a spiritual house, made not of bricks but of people – living stones. This is a beautiful, living, adapting, growing picture of what the Church is supposed to be. We are being 'built', with a sense of continual growth and development, never staying still.

And we are becoming 'a holy priesthood' in this living temple. A priest is a mediator between God and his people, who proclaims the words of God to his people, offers sacrifices to God and prays to God for his people. Peter calls the Church 'a holy priesthood' (v. 5). The Church, and every one of us within it, is called to proclaim the words of God to the world and to pray to God for the world. There is no longer a special group that does that: we are all called to do it. And we are to offer sacrifices to God, not blood sacrifices but ourselves. Being a *holy* priesthood is something that Jesus has done for us through his death on the cross, forgiving and cleansing us from our sins. But it is also something we choose to be too, aligning ourselves with a holy God and turning away from sinful ways to pursue God's ways.

When we realize the responsibility of being a holy priesthood, and when we reflect on all that Jesus has done for us to give us this privilege (see the verses before the 'therefore', in chapter 1), we recognize the call to live holy lives. To live a holy life requires us to make a daily choice to turn away from attitudes that destroy our inner lives. Peter calls us to 'Rid yourselves, therefore, of all malice, and all guile, insincerity, envy, and all slander', which turn dark thoughts into destructive words (v. 1). To rid ourselves means intentionally analysing our hearts and minds with the insight of the Holy Spirit. It means to put these attitudes aside at the beginning and end of each day.

One way to choose holiness is to fill your heart, your mind and your spirit with good things. When a baby is hungry, it cries out for its mother's breast milk, and that pure milk and intimacy with the mother satisfies all the baby's needs for growth and well-being. Peter calls followers of Jesus to 'long for the pure, spiritual milk' (v. 2). Why? For starters, we know it tastes good (v. 3), but we also know that, with spiritual food, we too can grow up into all the blessings and benefits of our salvation, the new life that Jesus has won for us through his death on the cross. Maturity for Christians comes from feeding on the word of God and prayer; it is choosing to love God, our neighbour and our fellow believers all the more; it is about living our lives for God, fulfilling God's purposes in the world rather than our own – offering our time, our money and our energy as a spiritual sacrifice acceptable to God through Jesus Christ (v. 5).

How do we do this? Peter has a simple but profound answer: by coming to Jesus (v. 4). Each day, we, the living stones, can come to him, *the* living Stone, our firm foundation, with gratitude in our hearts for our salvation and all that he has done for us. We can submit each part of our day to him: the decisions that we will make; the people we will see; and the challenges we will face. And when we come to him we know that he will satisfy our every need, strengthening us and helping us grow to maturity. Just as a newborn baby, full of its mother's milk, rests in its mother's arms, so we can rest in God, trusting him for all that lies ahead.

## Action

Bring any wrong attitudes, especially towards others, to Jesus and leave them at his feet. Ask Jesus to strengthen you as you pray and read the Scriptures. Bring the needs of the world to him today and ask for courage to speak for him today. Offer your day to him and pray that he will use you as you serve him, wherever you are.

## Prayer

Lord Jesus, thank you that you are building me into your spiritual house. Strengthen me more and more each day as I pray and as I read your word. May I bring glory to you today as I serve you in my thoughts and words and deeds. For the extension of your kingdom. Amen.

# 32

# Having the same love

If then there is any encouragement in Christ, any consolation from love, any sharing in the Spirit, any compassion and sympathy, make my joy complete: be of the same mind, having the same love, being in full accord and of one mind. Do nothing from selfish ambition or conceit, but in humility regard others as better than yourselves. Let each of you look not to your own interests, but to the interests of others. Let the same mind be in you that was in Christ Jesus,

>who, though he was in the form of God,
>>did not regard equality with God
>>as something to be exploited,
>but emptied himself,
>>taking the form of a slave,
>>being born in human likeness.
>And being found in human form,
>>he humbled himself
>>and became obedient to the point of death –
>>even death on a cross.

>Therefore God also highly exalted him
>>and gave him the name
>>that is above every name,

so that at the name of Jesus
    every knee should bend,
    in heaven and on earth and under the earth,
and every tongue should confess
    that Jesus Christ is Lord,
    to the glory of God the Father.
(Phil. 2.1–11)

Dietrich Bonhoeffer's writings are profound. In June 1944, as part of a series of poems from prison, he wrote the iconic poem 'Who Am I?' In it he asks the deep question of meaning and identity. Who am I? Am I the person whom the prison warders see, confident, cheerful and outwardly calm despite being imprisoned in a Nazi concentration camp? Or am I the person who hurts, a weakling, desperate for friends, birdsong and freedom? Bonhoeffer concludes that he is in fact both: he is a contradiction in terms who ultimately recognizes that he is God's, and this is all that counts.

Bonhoeffer's honesty is refreshing. He sees in his own brokenness and vanity that, for him to really flourish, he needs Jesus Christ. It is only in Jesus Christ that he can become fully himself. The outpouring of the Holy Spirit does not make us more and more like clones, but rather more beautiful and unique, made in God's image and liberated by God's extravagant grace.

St Paul is also in prison, as he writes his letter to the Christians in Philippi. Chapter 2 in his letter is a beautiful hymn to powerlessness and humility. Rather than echo the farewell discourses in John's Gospel, Paul reminds us that we are to make joy complete in one another. To do this, we must lay aside our vanity and self-indulgence, and strive for the common good. We must be clear of our motives and motivations so that we do not coerce or manipulate others for our own ends. Instead we are to regard others as better than ourselves and to be ready to support others' interests rather than pushing our own selfish ambition.

St Paul reminds us that our privilege in living the Christian life is to become more Christ-like, which means that we become more fully ourselves. It is God who empties himself, so that his people can become one with him. It is God who, through the cross, enables us to become citizens and co-heirs with Jesus of the kingdom of God.

This is an extraordinary act of powerlessness and humility, a wonderful act of generosity, whereby God places you at centre stage. It is because of you that God went to these great lengths. It is because of your brokenness and your confusion that God chooses to transform your flesh, to defeat your death and to bring you home. Therefore, despite the messiness of your day-to-day life, like Bonhoeffer, we can each add, 'Lord, I am thine'.

This self-emptying image is sometimes seen as the prayer of the desert. For centuries, Christians have taken to the desert to understand their humanity in places of nothingness. This is known as apophatic prayer, a prayer that seeks to be rid of all external stimuli, emptying the mind of words and ideas and simply resting in the presence of God. In this place, the searcher will find Jesus, who has self-emptied, who desires relationship and who loves the searcher. This is a quest for love, a quest for meaning and identity, wrapped not in vanity and self-delusion but with the clarity of nothingness. There are many desert fathers and mothers who can help shape this journey of discovery, but Charles de Foucauld may be helpful to us here. A Catholic priest and hermit in the nineteenth century, Charles was the founder of the Little Brothers of Jesus. His 'prayer of abandonment' contains powerful and painful imagery which has shaped many lives that were once gripped by vanity. The prayer of abandonment is a Lenten prayer, which you may like to make your own for the remaining days of Lent. These are words that St Paul and Dietrich Bonhoeffer might have grasped with enthusiasm.

## Action
Could you incorporate Foucauld's prayer of abandonment into different parts of your routine today, perhaps before a big task that you have to do, before you set off on a journey or as you prepare a meal?

## Prayer
Father,
I abandon myself into your hands;
do with me what you will.
Whatever you may do, I thank you:
I am ready for all, I accept all.
Let only your will be done in me,
and in all your creatures –
I wish no more than this, O Lord.
Into your hands I commend my soul:
I offer it to you with all the love of my heart,
for I love you, Lord, and so need to give myself,

to surrender myself into your hands without reserve,
and with boundless confidence,
for you are my Father.[1]

## Note

1 Charles de Foucauld, 'Prayer of Abandonment', <www.
brothercharles.org/wordpress/prayer-of-abandonment>.

Part 5

# LIVING A CHRIST-CENTRED LIFE

# 33

# Set your hope on the grace to be brought to you

Therefore prepare your minds for action; discipline yourselves; set all your hope on the grace that Jesus Christ will bring you when he is revealed. Like obedient children, do not be conformed to the desires that you formerly had in ignorance. Instead, as he who called you is holy, be holy yourselves in all your conduct.
(1 Pet. 1.13–15)

The question for those who received the letter we call 1 Peter was 'How do we survive under persecution?' They'd been scattered around the northern region of Asia Minor (modern-day Turkey). It felt as though God had deserted them. How were they to cope? This may not be our context, though it is of course the contemporary experience of many Christian believers throughout the world. It's also a letter that has a more definitive application for Christians whatever their circumstances.

In the first part of chapter 1, the focus has been on the hope that we inherit because of Jesus Christ's resurrection from the dead. From verse 13, there's a change of gear, to deal with the question 'If we have this hope, how should we then live?'

Throughout the New Testament, Paul and others have focused on the transformation of our minds as the key to Christian living. 'Prepare your minds for action,' says Peter (v. 13). The image is quite vivid – the ancient equivalent of rolling your sleeves up and putting your mind into gear. The antidote to being overtaken by the philosophy of contemporary society is to develop a Christian mind. That's difficult, for the materialism and scepticism of our culture militates against it – but we have to recognize that the Christian faith is pre-eminently counter-cultural – a challenge to the prevailing orthodoxy.

Peter then introduces the great Christian theme that is perhaps the hardest thing for us to get when it comes to Christian discipleship – the great Christian word *grace*: 'Set all your hope on the grace' that is in Jesus Christ (v. 13). We all find it hard to accept that there is nothing we can contribute to win our salvation, to put ourselves right with God. Our natural tendency is to want to assist God in making us his people, but the stark and wonderful truth is that it's all down to him! If I had a tenner for every person to whom I have explained the good news of Christ who has said to me, 'It can't be that simple', I would be very rich by now. But the simple message of the gospel is that, while we were sinners, Christ died for us (Rom. 5.8). All we can do is accept God's grace, forgiveness and love. When C. S. Lewis described his own conversion, the heart of his experience was that of finally admitting that he wasn't God and submitting to the one who was. He considered himself perhaps one of the most uneager new disciples in the country. It was only later that he saw the even deeper truth about God that this exposed. That the depth of his humility meant that even the most reticent convert was welcome.[1]

Once our minds are prepared for action and we know our dependence upon the grace of God, there is a call to 'be holy yourselves in all your conduct' (v. 15). The concept of holiness draws on the Old Testament background of being set apart for God (Peter quotes Leviticus in verse 16). But where the Old Testament understanding centred particularly on places, rituals and priests, the New Testament points us to an internalized way of living that applied to the Church as a whole (as inheritors of Old Testament Israel) but also to individuals. Our conduct is to be transformed as our minds have also been transformed – and this is a positive take on how our lives should be.

## Action

What do I most need to pray today? For my mind to be more conformed to that of Christ? For a greater dependence on grace? For a capacity to discover what it means to be holy in a situation that I find difficult and challenging?

## Prayer

Almighty God, who alone can bring order to the unruly wills and passions of the sinful: give us grace to love what you command and to desire what you promise, that in all the changes and chances of this fleeting world our hearts may surely be fixed where lasting joys are to be found, through Jesus Christ our Lord. Amen.

(Collect for the Third Sunday before Lent, *Common Worship*)

# Note

1 See C. S. Lewis, *Surprised by Joy* (London: HarperCollins, 2002), p. 266.

# 34

# He went off to a solitary place, where he prayed

In the morning, while it was still very dark, he got up and went out to a deserted place, and there he prayed. And Simon and his companions hunted for him. When they found him, they said to him, 'Everyone is searching for you.' He answered, 'Let us go on to the neighbouring towns, so that I may proclaim the message there also; for that is what I came out to do.' And he went throughout Galilee, proclaiming the message in their synagogues and casting out demons.
(Mark 1.35–39)

What keeps you up at night? What thoughts race around your mind when you are struggling to go to sleep, find rest, relax and stop? These are critical questions, as Christians, especially during Lent, take more seriously their duty to learn, pray and reflect on their walk with Jesus Christ. But it is not easy. The pressures of work, exciting job prospects, family responsibilities, a new birth, a friend's wedding, bereavement, a new opportunity or a new relationship can all add to a sense of unsettledness in our everyday lives. Like all people, Christians, when they are unsettled, will look to a myriad number of coping mechanisms to help them navigate extra stresses or stimuli. There are significant and growing levels of cocaine and caffeine in the water supply in London, according to a report published by King's College London in 2019,[1] which says something about the coping mechanisms we are using. Another study found that drugs are now available more quickly than a pizza delivery in parts of the capital through the use of county lines and the grooming of vulnerable young people.[2] Alcohol or pornography are also often used as a coping mechanism, and then, of course, there is addiction to work itself or to physical exercise.

So, how do you cope with extra stressors and strains when times are tough or joyful and abundant? The unsettling of our circumstances needs gentle negotiation, processing and perhaps a rootedness in our relationship with Jesus Christ so that we can get a better perspective.

The beginning of Mark's Gospel, like the rest of the Gospel is packed full of activity and action from chapter to chapter, and the first chapter is no exception. There is an enormous sense of expectation, something new exploding on to the scene. Jesus has already chosen a few disciples, healed a man with an evil spirit and Peter's mother-in-law, and the evening before healed all sorts of people from their diseases and sicknesses. Jesus has created a culture of relentless activity, where the first chosen disciples are high on adrenalin and eager for the next instalment. Jesus, however, tries to find solace and space. He shows us a sustainable pattern of ministry by going off to a deserted place to pray. Yet his silence is interrupted by a mob of followers, still intoxicated from the frenetic activity of the previous night. Mark states that Jesus was hunted down by Simon – it is an extraordinary expression, where he uses the Greek word κατεδίωξεν, meaning to follow closely and hunt down. It is the only time in the Gospels where this word is used. Knowing that their motivation is wrapped in their own vanity, Jesus calls time on Capernaum and introduces a mission to the neighbouring towns, so that he may proclaim his message there too. He then travels across Galilee proclaiming the message in the synagogues and casting out demons.

In this moment, Jesus does several things. First, he creates an expectation that an encounter with him changes people. Second, the mission belongs to him, and not to the disciples. Third, Jesus recognizes the impact that he is having upon others and upon their mental health, and therefore plans his ministry to take this into consideration. Finally, Jesus also shows a pattern for sustainable ministry by consciously seeking a place to pray and to be still amid all the activity.

Mark chapter 1 reminds us that encounters with Jesus will change people, and that there will be mixed reactions to this. It also reminds us that mission is intentional – we have to make deliberate decisions to engage with particular people. Jesus directs our efforts and our role is to join in. We are also reminded that, amid the complexities and stresses of our lives, it is good to find a quiet place to pray. Many see this as a luxury, but for Jesus it is a necessity.

## Action

Do we have any coping mechanisms that need changing? Are they life-enhancing or life-reducing?

## Prayer

Dear Lord, help me to find space to reflect, stop and pray. My life seems so full. I long to find helpful and edifying coping mechanisms because the ones I have used in the past have not always been the best for me or for others. Help me to use today as a gift from you, and help me find a sense of perspective in the busyness and confusion. Remind me today that I cannot be separated from your love. Amen.

## Notes

1 Thomas H. Miller et al., 'Biomonitoring of pesticides, pharmaceuticals and illicit drugs in a freshwater invertebrate to estimate toxic or effect pressure', *Environment International*, 129 (2019), pp. 595–606.

2 Adam R. Winstock, 'Cokeinoes! Cocaine delivered faster than pizza', Global Drug Survey, <www.globaldrugsurvey.com/gds-2018/cokeinoes-cocaine-delivered-faster-than-pizza>.

# 35

# Do the things you did at first

'To the angel of the church in Ephesus write: These are
the words of him who holds the seven stars in his right
hand, who walks among the seven golden lampstands:

"I know your works, your toil and your patient endurance. I know that you cannot tolerate evildoers;
you have tested those who claim to be apostles but are
not, and have found them to be false. I also know that
you are enduring patiently and bearing up for the sake
of my name, and that you have not grown weary. But
I have this against you, that you have abandoned the
love you had at first. Remember then from what you
have fallen; repent, and do the works you did at first.
If not, I will come to you and remove your lampstand
from its place, unless you repent. Yet this is to your
credit: you hate the works of the Nicolaitans, which
I also hate. Let anyone who has an ear listen to what
the Spirit is saying to the churches. To everyone who
conquers, I will give permission to eat from the tree of
life that is in the paradise of God."'
(Rev. 2.1–7)

We know quite a lot about the church in Ephesus. It was
on all accounts a famous church. It had been St Paul's
mission base for three years when the whole of western

155

Turkey was evangelized. Luke wrote in Acts 19 about their disciple-making, their community transformation their church-planting all over the region. Paul wrote the letter to them about being in Christ, about unity, marriage and prayer. St John the Apostle was a bishop there, looking after Mary, mother of Jesus, before he was exiled by the Roman emperor to Patmos. What then became of the church at Ephesus? By the time these words were written, some thirty years later, the church had lost something vital.

Jesus, speaking through John's letter to the church, describes their great deeds (being kind and generous and making a difference in their city), their great doctrine (knowing the truth about Jesus and exposing false and dangerous teaching) and their great perseverance, in spite of discrimination against them. Then comes a 'but'. When you hear a list of good things and then a 'but', it's the 'but' that you really need to listen to. And that seems to be the case here too. Despite all their great deeds, they had lost sight of the great God who should have been the motivating force for all of them: they had lost their first love.

We are called to love God with all our heart, mind, soul and strength because we were made to have a deep and loving connection with God. Paul had taught the Ephesians that they were to be 'in Christ'. They were to find their purpose, their life, their love, their joy, their peace and their authority in him, through an intimate, personal, life-giving relationship with the living God. And somewhere along the way they had missed this.

How is that possible? It is so easy to get caught up in the *what* that we miss out on the *who*, to focus so much on doctrine that we miss out on Jesus. If you just do good deeds without the love of God flowing in and through you, you miss out on sharing the most important part of our faith, of helping others to discover the deepest and most important relationship they will ever experience.

How can we recover our first love? 'Remember' how your faith came alive in the first place, Jesus says (v. 5). It was not for anything you did, but it was because of what Jesus did for you and how he revealed himself to you. '*Repent*' over lost love, Jesus says (v. 5). Where are you with God? How are your worship, your prayer life, your devotional life? Where is the passion that you have lost? Acknowledge that you have lost it. Say sorry, ask for forgiveness and then come to him. Paul prayed for the Ephesians (3.14–19) that they would have the power to strengthen their faith and the power to grasp his love. It is out of the overflow of this love that we are to *do* good works, to love our neighbours and to serve others with the hands and feet of Jesus.

So, what happened to that church? A letter was written to the church of Ephesus by Bishop Ignatius twenty years later:

I gave a godly welcome to your church which has so endeared itself to us by reason of your upright nature, marked as it is by faith in Jesus Christ, our Saviour, and by love of him. You are imitators of God; and it was God's blood that stirred you up once more to do the sort of thing you do naturally and have now done to perfection . . . In God's name, therefore, I received your large congregation in the person of Onesimus, your bishop in the world, a man whose love is beyond words.[1]

They found their first love again, led by a bishop who was once a runaway slave and was led to Christ by Paul, who returned to his former master Philemon, and who went on to live out the life of love he had received from Jesus.

## Action

Turn to Jesus in prayer and *remember* how much he loves you, *repent* of any love lost and choose to *do* something for someone today that flows from that love.

Cultivate your devotional life, praying for God's love to fill you each day and reading and reflecting on Jesus in the Scriptures. Join a Bible study group in your church and intentionally grow with others.

## Prayer

Lord Jesus, thank you for loving me, for the love I see in the cross on which you died. Forgive me for my lack of love. Kindle that love afresh in my heart today that I might overflow with love by the power of your Spirit. Amen.

## Note

1 *Early Christian Fathers*, ed. Cyril C. Richardson (Westminster Press, 1953), p. 88, <www.ccel.org/ccel/richardson/fathers.vi.ii.iii.i.html>.

# 36

# If we confess our sins he is faithful

If we say that we have no sin, we deceive ourselves, and the truth is not in us. If we confess our sins, he who is faithful and just will forgive us our sins and cleanse us from all unrighteousness. If we say that we have not sinned, we make him a liar, and his word is not in us. (1 John 1.8–10)

Perhaps the best-known parable of Jesus as set down in the Gospels is one of those found in St Luke's Gospel, chapter 15. We usually know it as the parable of the prodigal son, though sometimes it is called the parable of the loving or forgiving father. In the story, the younger of two sons demands his share of his father's inheritance (effectively rendering the father dead in his sight), runs away, spends all the money and ends up in penury and servitude. Coming to his senses, he returns home. The father rushes out to greet him, and his son says to him, 'Father, I have sinned against heaven and before you' (Luke 15.18). The father puts a robe on his back and a ring on his finger, kills the fatted calf and throws a splendid feast to celebrate their reconciliation.

In the story, Jesus teaches us that his Father in heaven is a God of mercy and forgiveness. The parable describes how the son repents – but, interestingly, the father in the story hurries to greet and embrace his son even before he has had a chance to hear him confess his sin.

Early Christians understood repentance to be an essential part of what it means to follow Jesus but they also had a puzzle to solve. Baptism, the early Church believed, not only brought regeneration into a new life in Christ, but also washed away sin. How were they to deal with the reality that, even after baptism, Christians were prone to commit sin? Was this sin unforgivable? Gradually Christians came to the view that even post-baptismal sin, when it was confessed, could be absolved, and the penitent sinner restored to full fellowship and communion with the Church.

The author of the first letter of John makes three things plain: first, the reality of sin – 'all have sinned, and fall short of the glory of God', as St Paul writes (Rom. 3.23); second, God's desire to forgive; and, third, the danger of denying our own sin.

Every principal Christian liturgy, be that Morning or Evening Prayer or the celebration of the Eucharist, begins with or contains an act of corporate confession on the part of those joining together for worship. We may, of course, name our sins before God in the secrecy of our own hearts and in our private prayers, and trust in God's forgiveness when we are penitent. However, in addition to these corporate and private means of bringing our sins and failings before the Lord, the Church offers her members the assurance of God's forgiveness through sacramental confession, also called the sacrament of reconciliation or penance, where we confess our sins aloud to God in the presence of a priest. Having heard this confession and a sincere expression of repentance, the priest offers spiritual guidance and advice and assures the person who has made their confession that God forgives them and absolves them from their sins. By virtue of his ordination, the priest is authorized on behalf of the whole Christian community to declare the forgiveness of sins. Anglican ordination services have always stressed this aspect of priestly ministry, derived from the words of Jesus spoken to the apostles in St John's Gospel, chapter 20. But it is God who forgives – it is God (as represented by the father in the parable) who rushes out to meet us, welcoming us home and reconciling us to himself.

There is much more that could be said about sacramental confession than the space here allows. There is much helpful material available to assist with making a first confession, if that is something you feel prompted to do. The great German theologian and martyr Dietrich Bonhoeffer called confession 'the renewal of the joy of baptism'.[1] Certainly it is a means of grace and of restoration, an encounter with our merciful and loving Father in heaven.

## Action

Spend some time examining your life as a disciple of Jesus, perhaps with the Beatitudes (Matt. 5: 1–12) to assist you with your reflection. Prepare to make confession of your sins, perhaps before Easter or Christmas, or a significant moment or event in your life. Know that God longs to heal, to forgive and to restore you to himself.

## Prayer

A prayer of John Wesley (1703–1791):

Forgive them all, O Lord:
our sins of omission and our sins of commission;
the sins of our youth and the sins of our riper
    years;
the sins of our souls and the sins of our bodies;
our secret and more open sins;
our sins of ignorance and surprise,
and our more deliberate and presumptuous sin;
the sins we have done to please ourselves
and the sins we have done to please others;
the sins we know and remember,
and the sins we have forgotten;
the sins we have striven to hide from others
and the sins by which we have made others
    offend;
forgive them, O Lord, forgive them all for his
    sake,
who died for our sins and rose for our
    justification,
and now stands at thy right hand to make
    intercession for us,
Jesus Christ our Lord.[2]

## Notes

1 Rowan Williams, *God with Us* (London: SPCK, 2017), p. 4.

2 Williams, *God with Us*, p. 4.

# 37

# Love your enemies

'You have heard that it was said, "You shall love your neighbour and hate your enemy." But I say to you, Love your enemies and pray for those who persecute you, so that you may be children of your Father in heaven; for he makes his sun rise on the evil and on the good, and sends rain on the righteous and on the unrighteous. For if you love those who love you, what reward do you have? Do not even the tax-collectors do the same? And if you greet only your brothers and sisters, what more are you doing than others? Do not even the Gentiles do the same? Be perfect, therefore, as your heavenly Father is perfect.'
(Matt. 5.43–48)

Polarization and partisanship have been poisoning public discourse over the last few years. It has become all too easy to see those who think differently from us as being on the 'wrong' side of the argument, while we sit comfortably on the 'right' side. A sense of ideological superiority can often lead to a sense of moral superiority. 'I am right', and 'they are wrong' becomes 'I am good' and 'they are bad'. Sadly, this slippery slope has led, in some cases, to hate speech and aggressive isolation of those who hold different views.

It is not surprising that such a hostile climate encourages us to hunker down and consolidate our sense of belonging within our own communities. But by so doing we compound the problem, setting ourselves apart from those around us. For example, it can sometimes seem that there is a growing disinclination to welcome strangers or refugees. The idea of making space for a stranger seems, for many, vastly removed from our reality, a naive hope.

The Church is not exempt from the danger of distancing itself from others. The very language of faith – for example, 'redemption', 'salvation' and 'sinner' – sets up explicit and implicit categories of who is 'in' and who is 'out'. But this is not the whole story. If polarization is the poison, Christ's call to love our enemies is the antidote to that poison.

Rabbi Jonathan Sacks has said that he used to think that the most important line in the Bible was 'love your neighbour as yourself' (Matt. 22.39), but he came to realize that it is easy to love your neighbour because they are quite like yourself. What is hard is to love the stranger, the one whose ethnicity, culture or creed is different from yours. How, then, do we begin to love in a way that transcends the boundaries we are so quick to put up? How do we allow the antidote of love to have its full effect? This is where Jesus' call to love even our enemies comes in.

The call to 'love your enemies and pray for those who persecute you' (Matt. 5.44) requires that we transcend our tribal loyalties. The reason for this is notable: 'so that you may be children of your Father in heaven; for he makes his sun rise on the evil and the good' (v. 45). Despite the fact that there are clear polarities in the mind of God, these do not set the boundaries for his merciful care of all who are made in his image.

The idea that the image of God is a fundamental part of all human identity is central to the Christian faith. Rooted as it is in creation (Gen. 1.27), it sheds light on one reason why God is willing to provide so generously for those beyond his covenant people (v. 45). All human life is intrinsically valuable.

Our challenge is not to pretend that we are all alike: clearly we are not. But to recognize that and hopefully learn in some small way to overcome our intrinsic nature, which pushes others away and tries to carve out territory for ourselves. Instead we are to see our context through the eyes of God. Might it help us to love our enemies if we remember that they too are made in the image of God?

C. S. Lewis reminded us that we should never consider anyone insignificant, because their future state is so *extraordinarily significant*. If we were able to see what God's people will one day be, our instinct would be awe rather than avoidance. For we will all be resplendent, beyond earthly imagining.[1] Might we be slower to speak, quicker to listen and slower to become angry at those who think differently from us if we remember their worth? Lewis said that our love has to be real and cost us, because our neighbour is the holiest thing there is after the Blessed Sacrament. Let us strive, with the help of God, to see as God sees and so to love as God loves.

## Action

Who will you meet today? Pray that God will help you to see them as he does, so that you listen to them more intently and speak to them more generously.

## Prayer

Lord, you have taught us
that all our doings without love are nothing worth:
send your Holy Spirit and pour into our hearts
that most excellent gift of love,
the true bond of peace and of all virtues,
without which whoever lives is counted dead before
    you.
Grant this for your only Son Jesus Christ's sake,
who is alive and reigns with you,
in the unity of the Holy Spirit, one God,
now and for ever. Amen.
(Collect for the Second Sunday after Trinity,
    *Common Worship*)

## Note

1 See C. S. Lewis, 'The Weight of Glory', in *The Weight of Glory and Other Addresses* (Grand Rapids, MI: Zondervan, 2001), pp. 45–6.

# 38

# Deny yourself, take up your cross and follow me

He called the crowd with his disciples, and said to them, 'If any want to become my followers, let them deny themselves and take up their cross and follow me. For those who want to save their life will lose it, and those who lose their life for my sake, and for the sake of the gospel, will save it. For what will it profit them to gain the whole world and forfeit their life? Indeed, what can they give in return for their life? Those who are ashamed of me and of my words in this adulterous and sinful generation, of them the Son of Man will also be ashamed when he comes in the glory of his Father with the holy angels.'
(Mark 8.34–38)

What good is it to gain the whole world and yet lose your soul in the process? Jesus' question is telling, repeated in some of the great myths of Western culture, such as the story of Faust and his pact with the devil. Yet it doesn't have to be as dramatic as that – it can describe all kinds of smaller, petty decisions we make, when we are lured by the initial pull of something that makes us ignore the darker consequences further down the line.

Jesus answers his own question with three simple, pithy statements that point the way to saving our souls, or guarding our hearts. First, *deny yourself*. In a culture that tells us to be ourselves, to be kind to ourselves, to indulge ourselves or even to market ourselves, this is deeply counter-cultural. It's important, however, to think of which 'self' Jesus is referring to. In an earlier reflection in this book on Romans 6, we considered Paul's idea of our two 'selves': the old self that was buried in baptism and the new self that rose again with Christ, 'created in Christ Jesus for good works' (Eph. 2.10). Denying ourselves is recognizing the inner voice that wants to be the centre of attention, that *self* – and being ruthless with it. It doesn't mean abusing ourselves – there is a proper kind of self-regard and self-care that makes sure we look after ourselves well enough to care for others and to enjoy the good gifts of God, but unless we learn how to discipline that self-centred nagging voice inside, we won't get very far in the spiritual life.

Second, *take up your cross*. Each of us has things in our life that, like Jesus and his cross, we would dearly love not to have to carry and to be able to lay down, but for one reason or another we can't do that. Maybe it's an ongoing illness, a broken relationship, a difficult marriage, the cost of a calling God has placed on us or a repeated temptation that won't go away. We pray for change, we seek justice, yet sometimes these things cannot be removed. The wisdom of Jesus is that there may come a time when we just have to carry it, as he did, until the day God takes it away, in this life or the next. We have to look at it as Jesus did the cross, as something temporary and painful, but through which God may be able to do far more than we could ever imagine. So often it is through these very things that God changes us. It is not despite our brokenness, but precisely out of our brokenness, that God reaches out to others. It is only as we reach out to others as fellow strugglers, fellow sinners and fellow failures that we can do them any lasting good.

Third, *follow me*. To follow Jesus is to become his apprentice, his student. A disciple of a rabbi would listen to his every word, watch his every move and try to imitate him until it became second nature. Eventually, such a following meant not so much slavish obedience as getting into the mindset and attitudes of the master so that when the disciple faced new situations that the master himself had not faced before, the disciple would be able to do what his teacher would have done.

This is the paradox of the Christian life. It looks like death, like a path to a funeral, but it is in fact the way to life: 'those who want to save their life will lose it, and those who lose their life for my sake will save it' (Matt. 16.25).

George MacDonald once wrote:

There is no forgetting of ourselves but in the finding of our deeper, our true self – God's idea of us when he devised us – the Christ in us. Nothing but that self can displace the false, greedy, whining Self, of which most of us are so fond and proud.[1]

Can you think of a person more alive than Jesus Christ – or his saints on earth? These are people who have begun to find their true selves, their Christ-like selves. That is what we are invited to do on this path of discipleship. There is only one simple way to be reborn: to deny ourselves, take up our cross and follow Jesus.

## Action

What is God calling you to deny yourself? Where do you need to be ruthless with your inner voice that wants to be the centre of attention?

## Prayer

Dear Father, your son Jesus invites me to lose my life for his sake. I confess that I find that hard. I cling on to my old self and fear letting go. Help me to live out of my new identity in Christ, to take up my cross this day and to follow Jesus wherever he leads. Amen.

## Note

1 George MacDonald, *Sir Gibbie*, <www.fullbooks.com/Sir-Gibbie4.html>.

# 39

# Seek peace and pursue it

Finally, all of you, have unity of spirit, sympathy, love for one another, a tender heart, and a humble mind. Do not repay evil for evil or abuse for abuse; but, on the contrary, repay with a blessing. It is for this that you were called – that you might inherit a blessing. For

'Those who desire life
and desire to see good days,
let them keep their tongues from evil
and their lips from speaking deceit;
let them turn away from evil and do good;
let them seek peace and pursue it.
For the eyes of the Lord are on the righteous,
and his ears are open to their prayer.
But the face of the Lord is against those who
do evil.'

(1 Pet. 3.8–12)

The story is told of a soldier who, after a hard day training at the barracks, would pick up his Bible to read and pray at the end of every evening. Many in his company mocked and incessantly insulted him for this. One night, as the jeers began to escalate, one of the men picked up his boots, soiled and muddy from the day's activities and threw them at the soldier as he struggled to read. It is a terrible picture: his clothes covered with mud, his dignity disregarded, and all because he was simply trying to practise his religion.

Many of us will never have experienced this kind of hostility towards our faith. We are blessed to live in a part of the world that champions freedom of religion and freedom of speech. Many Christians in many parts of the world face open and active persecution in ways we cannot even imagine. And yet there may be subtle ways in which we can experience being sidelined or silenced. These include awkward relationships in families, the choices others make about who they invite to social events after work or even the people towards whom they gravitate at the coffee break. We may feel passed over in all kinds of ways. How do we respond to this?

The temptation, as St Peter points out, is for us to repay 'evil for evil', to find subtle ways of administering our own retribution. But Peter calls us to something higher, something heavenly. He asks us to repay evil 'with a blessing'. The story of the Christian soldier with which I began contains a remarkable example of this. When the soldier who had thrown the boots woke up the next morning, he found the muddy boots that he had thrown across the room gleaming and clean at the foot of his bed. The objects that he had thrown in anger had been gently replaced with love. The Christian had not repaid 'evil for evil' but 'with a blessing'.

The type of evil Peter is writing about in this letter clearly takes the form of verbal insults directed at the community of faith. He speaks of being 'maligned' 'for your good conduct in Christ', (v. 16) and 'reviled for the name of Christ'

(4.14). So we need to be clear that the blessing Peter encourages us to extend is in the context of verbal insult rather than any kind of physical abuse. That cannot be tolerated, and Peter himself calls us to make use of the authorities so that justice might be done (2.14). How we should respond to verbal insults to our faith is, however, radically different from the world around us.

The reason for responding in such a way is surprising: it is so that we will 'inherit a blessing'. What does this mean? As noted in my earlier reflection on 1 Peter 1, our hope is a gift through God's great mercy, because we have been sprinkled by Christ's blood on the cross (1 Peter 1.2). Our salvation is not earned but a gift. Peter is not arguing that we earn our inheritance but that our behaviour bears witness to the inheritance that we have already been given. As we show mercy to those who offend us, we show the world the family way of those who have been born again.

But there is a second, captivating motivation for this as well: knowing that the 'eyes of the Lord' are gazing on us and that 'his ears are open' to us (v. 12). Peter is talking about a deep sense of communion with God. This is what it means to know 'life' and 'see good days' (v. 10). This is what it is like to live with a felt sense of God close to us. Peter's promise is that, as we persevere in loving our enemies, we will experience a deep sense of the love of God.

## Action

How can you seek to engage again with someone who has seemed to scorn your faith? Could you reach out to a family member, friend or colleague with a note of encouragement?

## Prayer

We praise you for our new birth into a living hope and inheritance that can never perish, spoil or fade. Help us, Father, in the power of the spirit, to live in a manner worthy of Christ. When we are maligned, misquoted or misunderstood let our tone reflect that of Jesus. Grant that we may mirror his grace to us that others might glimpse your face. Amen.

# 40

# Let perseverance finish its work

> My brothers and sisters, whenever you face trials of any
> kind, consider it nothing but joy, because you know
> that the testing of your faith produces endurance; and
> let endurance have its full effect, so that you may be
> mature and complete, lacking in nothing.
> (James 1.2–4)

'Resilience' is something of a buzz word. In recent times, social thinkers have observed the importance of people being able to adapt well in the face of adversity and to bounce back from difficult experiences. We have had to learn again the value of practising self-care, staying connected to others and trying to find purpose and meaning in life, even when things are tough. Business has also seen the need for resilience training – not just to help organizations be adaptable, but to bolster individuals, perhaps to enable them to be more economically productive members of the workforce.

When James writes of facing trials with joy and of cultivating endurance, he is recommending an attitude of courageous and patient hope. Such an attitude may be helpful to Christians as they seek to live their lives in a resilient fashion, enduring adversity in the knowledge that they are members in Christ of God's resurrection people. But something else is at work in James's epistle. Throughout the letter James stresses the holiness of the poor, and offers a challenge to the rich to set aside their wealthy and entitled ways of behaving and turn to the good works that will demonstrate their belief that all are one in Christ. In these early verses, his use of the Greek word *hypomone* does not denote an endurance that is passive or powerless in the face of unjust social or economic structures. Rather, it implies a different kind of patience and readiness, one that resists evil, plots a different path and waits for the right moment to make a hopeful strike for justice. Patience does not justify or support exploitation; it is called to actively work against it.

James emphasizes the common humanity we share when he addresses his hearers as *adelphoi*. When we are truly brothers and sisters in Christ we are not called to look out for our own (family, kinship group or local community) but to see all people in their full stature as children of God. Against the violent background of Roman Judea in the decade before James was killed (AD 62), his call to let endurance have its full effect means standing in solidarity as brothers and sisters against corruption, injustice and poverty. Individual resilience may have its place in the journey of life, but embracing a life of faith means seeking righteousness, justice and peace, with integrity of belief and action, across social structures. This is a peaceful movement but one that is no less active and purposeful for its foundation in faith.

'Resilience' as a term originated in materials science and is used to describe the degree to which objects can spring back into shape. James asks us to consider not only how resilient we are as individuals, but whether the structures that we share – family, society, government and economic systems – are shaped in such a way as to allow each member to be 'mature and complete, lacking in nothing'. To be formed in such a way that no one need be stretched beyond their capacity and no human being need reach a point of no return involves fair wages and working conditions, as well as caring collectively for those who are vulnerable and without the natural bonds of support.

Faith in Jesus Christ, through his suffering, death and resurrection, makes us look beyond individual productivity and resilience to seek God's justice across the gossamer-fine threads of society. Are we ready and waiting to spin the web of God's kingdom across the earth?

## Action

Ask yourself if your actions contribute to others' resilience or wear it down. At work, do you look to build others up or to put them down? If you employ a cleaner, do you pay them the living wage? Are you willing to support someone who is making a principled stand against injustice and trying to improve things for others, or do you choose to look the other way? Choose one thing that you will do this Lent to contribute to improving someone else's resilience. Pledge to stick with it in the longer term as part of belonging to God's Easter community of hope.

## Prayer

God of all hope,
you weave your love around us
with threads that connect and support.
Help us to endure the trials of life

and the testing of our faith
knowing that you hold us safe.
In gratitude, let us strengthen the webs of
    community
so that filaments of love may surround the
    vulnerable,
and remind us that we are bound together in Christ.
Amen.